A Farm Near Frohna

The Story Behind a Missouri Century Farm

Kaempfe-Koenig Family History and Genealogy

Mary Linda Miller

mary linda miller
Orlando, Florida
www.marylindamiller.com

Library of Congress Cataloging Information
LC Control Number 2011282309

Miller, Mary Linda 1947—
    A farm near Frohna: the story behind a Missouri century farm
    Kaempfe-Koenig family history and genealogy
    Orlando, Fla: Mary Linda Miller, © 2010

    i, 94 p. : ill., maps, ports. ; 26 cm.
    Includes bibliographical references (p. 84-88) and index.
    1. Kemp family. 2. Koenig family. 3. German Americans—Genealogy.
4. Farm life—Missouri—Perry County—Anecdotes. 5. Frohna (Mo.)—Genealogy.
6. Perry County (Mo.)—Genealogy.
CS71.K346 2010   RG 929.2 KAEMPFE KOENIG   (OCoLC)ocn676758168
ISBN-13: 9781453707838 (softcover)
ISBN-10: 1453707832 (softcover)

Published in the U.S.A.
Mary Linda Miller
Orlando, Florida
www.marylindamiller.com

DEDICATION

For Mel and Jason
The greatest guys in the world
Both truly wonderful Kaempfe-Koenig descendants

"..you are no longer foreigners and aliens, but fellow citizens with God's people.."
Ephesians 2:19

Disclaimer

Large portions of the text and many illustrations, maps and photographs appeared in a 53-page booklet titled "The Genealogy of Carmelo Louis Monti and His Ancestral History" by Mary Linda Miller. Each of the original eight copies bore the names of each of his five siblings or two parents in lieu of his name, and they were published on © September 11, 2003; subsequent copies were distributed to select family members in 2003 or thereafter; but the booklet was never offered for sale to the public. This new book represents a considerable revision to that material, in part because it focuses on only one of Carmelo's parent's ancestry. It includes numerous corrections, substantial new text, additional illustrations, and photographs, and revised ancestor and descendant charts.

I make no guarantees that the material contained herein is accurate or complete, although I did attempt to make it so. Errors abound in the documents I obtained, especially spelling errors and conflicting dates. Many names and dates were provided to me in the form of handwritten notes or were the product of other genealogists' research; although I have verified many, others have not been or cannot be documented. Recollections, even eyewitness accounts, by a variety of living people conflicted with other versions of the same story from other sources, whether people, books, Internet, or newspapers. I weighed the variations and chose the one that seemed most plausible, and in many places I indicate where that happens. I have used the words "maybe" or "probably" or "likely" to indicate various levels of speculation, all my subjective opinion.

At any generation level there could be children not shown because they were not documented in anything available to me. Living persons' data has been reduced to "name only" for their privacy. The use of an asterisk next to a name (*) indicates that there is only one Internet source for the name, and it is unverified by other means. The author specifically disclaims any responsibility for any liabilities, loss, or risk, personal or otherwise, which is incurred as a consequence, directly or indirectly, of the use and application of any of the contents of this book.

Any omission of credit is purely unintentional and should not be construed as plagiarism or copyright infringement. See Bibliography for additional credits.

ACKNOWLEDGMENTS

Researching and writing this was a great adventure, but I could not have done it without help. Thanks are in order to numerous people.

1. Milda (Kaempfe) Monti for writing down many names and dates in 1986 and mailing it to her son Carmelo in Phoenix, AZ, and for starting me on this journey.

2. Carmelo Monti, my husband, for encouraging this obsession with the luxurious gift of time; for contributing numerous drawings of maps, the church in Korbussen, and city crests; and for his advice on the cover and page design.

3. My deepest gratitude to Courtney Meyer and Imogene (Meyer) Unger for their time and generosity in sharing their considerable knowledge of the farm and early days in Frohna and, to Imy, for sending so many photographs.

4. A special note of thanks to Sheila Monti-Molina for handling the photographs for the Milda (Kaempfe) Monti Estate and for making copies and distributing them to family members.

5. Others who have provided names, dates, photographs, or other material include Morgan (Meyr) Lake, Nelson Haertling, Cindy (Bachmann) Brigham, Shannon Ryan, Eric Kreft, T. V. Vessell, Sheila Monti-Molina, Paul Monti, and Charles Monti Jr.

6. My son Jason Monti for solving my computer problems and for teaching me so many new things.

7. All of the sources in my bibliography, from which this document is derived.

TABLE OF CONTENTS

Germany 1815

Three Regions From Which Eight German Ancestors Emigrated

Map drawn by Carmelo L. Monti

INTRODUCTION

In 1998, Imogene and Jerry Unger received the Missouri Century Farm Award after documenting that their farm near Frohna, Missouri had been in the family for over a hundred years. Indeed, the farm has been owned by one Kaempfe or another since December 7, 1876 when Traugott Kaempfe bought it from Robert M. Smith and moved his family from Millstadt, Illinois to Frohna. Traugott's roots in Missouri ran much deeper than that, as he had been born in Altenburg, Missouri to German immigrants who had traveled across the Atlantic as part of the Stephanites (later called the Gesellshaft), a group of conservative Lutheran religious zealots seeking freedom.

Traugott's son Theodor married Lina Koenig from another local German family, and eventually the couple bought the farm from Traugott's heirs after his death. Finally, their granddaughter Imogene, who has lived most of her life in Frohna and spent a good portion of her childhood on the farm, and her husband Jerry bought the land from Theodor's heirs.

The story seems simple enough. They were all German. They lived in Missouri and raised families there, and the farm passed down through the generations.

But research on their family tree revealed a much more complex and interesting picture. It was a richly textured story with familiar sounding city names scattered across Germany and ships' registries that offered both clues and mysteries. There was a harrowing voyage across the ocean, a steamship ride up the Mississippi, religious persecution, a lawsuit, and wills. There were entrepreneurial activities of all sorts and homesteading when Missouri was a barely-new state. There were orphans and Civil War tragedy. There were too many women who died young and too many children who died in infancy. There was death by diseases of every sort, a record-breaking tornado, and the extinction of one ancestral line in the German homeland.

Kaempfe and Koenig forebears were a mixed group of central Europeans leaving behind religious persecution and economic turmoil. Some of them helped to establish the foundation for the Lutheran Church—Missouri Synod, and they continued to speak German for several generations in their insulated small communities. Their descendants' stories are mostly rural, with four generations or more tilling the land in Missouri and Illinois before the next three generations began to scatter with some going to other states or the city to seek opportunity.

The story of the Kaempfe farm—and all of the people who came and went, those who enjoyed the fruits of its soil and who grew and thrived there—that story represents real American history at its best. But the tale really began in Germany, when, during the middle of the nineteenth century, from 1840 to 1890, four million Germans immigrated to the United States, among them all eight people who were the grandparents of Theodor Kaempfe and Lina Koenig. Those ancestors came from three different regions, as depicted on the adjacent map of Germany as it appeared in 1815: (1) **Duchy of Saxony**—three small towns in the area around Dresden; (2) **Prussia**—two small towns in the Hanover province of the Kingdom of Prussia; and (3) **Thuringia**—three small agricultural villages in the Duchy of Saxe-Altenburg which is part of Thuringia. A glance at an ancestry or descendants chart shows that in most cases their dates of birth and death and cities of origin are known. For some, there are enough details to construct a small picture of their lives, but none as complete as for the Kaempfes. For others, few details exist so curiosity gives rise to speculation.

They probably all share the common history of their regions, which is not common at all. It is a history rife with the warfare of ancient tribes, kings and nobles, and religious factions. Excavations in some of the villages have revealed Iron Age artifacts from a time when various Teutonic peoples vied for land. Those tribes attempted invasions of Italy but were beaten back and subjugated by the Roman Caesar. Revolts and annihilation of Ceasar's armies eventually lead to their withdrawal by Augustus around 9 A.D. By this time there were four classes of people: nobles from whence kings arose; freemen who held property; freedmen who held no property but could farm land at the nobles' discretion; and slaves. Their religion was polytheist, and they worshiped Thor, Woden and Tyr, among others. Oddly, they erected no temples and had no idols, but did believe in life after death and eternal justice. Recorded history for the specific towns of origin began a few hundred years later.

Following is a list of the ancestors and their towns of origin, which will be discussed at greater length in Parts One and Two.

Part One: Kaempfe-Hennecke

Parents of Theodor Samuel Kaempfe

Traugott Gotthilf Kaempfe	Altenburg, Perry County, Missouri
Justine Engel Hennecke	Centreville, St. Clair County, Illinois

Grandparents of Theodor Samuel Kaempfe

Johann Samuel Gottfried Kaempfe	Rippien, Dresden, Saxony, Germany
Johanna Juliane Christiane Lippisch	Kleinpestitz, Dresden, Saxony, Germany
Heinrich Hennecke	Vogelbeck, Hanover, Prussia, Germany
Engell Christine Justina Tute	Odagsen, Hanover, Prussia, Germany

Part Two: Koenig-Reuschel

Parents of Lina Christina Koenig

Edward Wilhelm Koenig	Frohna, Perry County, Missouri
Juliana Mathilda Reuschel	Brazeau Township, Perry County, Missouri

Grandparents of Lina Christina Koenig

Andreas Koenig	Korbussen, Sax-Altenburg, Thuringia, Germany
Christina Justina Haertling	Poeppeln, Saxe-Altenburg, Thuringia, Germany
Friederick Bernhardt Reuschel	Scheosswieths, Seesen, Altenburg, Germany
Friederika Emilia Siermann	Heukewalde, Saxe-Altenburg, Thuringia, Germany

Their family histories, genealogy, and the pages of this book are divided between those two distinct family groups, determined by the surnames of Theodor's parents (Kaempfe-Hennecke) and Lina's parents (Koenig-Reuschel). Some of this material was originally found in the second half of a two-part booklet first produced in 2003. For this expanded book-length version I have added new illustrations by Carmelo Monti, many more photos from the collections of Imogene (Meyer) Unger and the Milda (Kaempfe) Monti Estate, and one new section—Part Three—that focuses on the twentieth century generation—those Kaempfe siblings born between 1900 and 1930 who were Theodor's and Lina's children. Each of their stories was produced with help from Imy Unger, Courtney Meyer, and Carmelo Monti, all contributing detailed stories of their parents' early lives, and anecdotes from their childhoods about their aunts and uncles, all of which paints a lovely picture of life on a farm near Frohna.

Theodor Samuel Kaempfe and Lina Christina Koenig
Married November 8, 1906
Photo courtesy of Miller-Monti Collection

Traugott Gotthilf and Justine Engel (Hennecke) Kaempfe
Circa 1906
Traugott and Justine bought the farm near Frohna, Missouri in 1876
Photo courtesy of Milda (Kaempfe) Monti Estate

PART ONE

KAEMPFE - HENNECKE

Heraldic Symbols for Two Ancestral Towns

Rippien

This heraldic symbol represents two historical economic enterprises traditionally found in the town of Rippien, Germany: farming and stone quarries. The sandstone was depleted around 1900, but even today agriculture remains important. Rippien, near Dresden, was likely the birthplace of Samuel Kaempfe (Traugott's father).

Kleinpestitz

This is the municipal seal of Kleinpestitz, Germany and is derived from a seal found above a yard entry gate dating to 1777 in a complex of well-preserved farmhouses that originally belonged to the Palitzsch family. Juliane Lippisch (Traugott's mother) was born in this town, and the Kaempfe family emigrated from there.

Ancestors of Theodor Samuel KAEMPFE

Samuel Gottfried KAEMPFE(*) (b.Abt 1785-Germany;m.Abt 1810)

Johann Samuel Gottfried KAEMPFE (b.12 Oct 1811-Rippien,Dresden,Saxony,Germany;m.5 Feb 1837;d.9 Jun 1879-Millstadt IL)

Missis KAEMPFE(*) (b.Abt 1789-Germany)

Traugott Gotthilf KAEMPFE (b.10 Aug 1840-Altenburg,Perry Co.,MO;m.7 May 1865;d.11 Dec 1909-Frohna,Perry Co.,MO)

Adam LIPPISCH(*) (b.1699-Doelzschen,Dresden,Saxony,Germany;m.Abt 1725;d.31 Mar 1762)

Johann George LIPPISCH(*) (b.22 Sep 1726-Doelzschen,Germany;m.23 Apr 1749;d.31 Mar 1760-Doelzschen,Germany)

Martha UNKNOWN(*) (b.5 Aug 1701-Doelzschen,Dresden,Saxony,Germany;d.15 Oct 1758)

Johann Gottlieb LIPPISCH(*) (b.28 Sep 1751-Doelzschen,Germany;m.Abt 1776;d.7 Jul 1817-Dresden,Saxony,Germany)

Peter RUEHLE(*) (b.Abt 1700-Germany;m.Abt 1725)

Maria RUEHLE(*) (b.1726-Gostritz,Saxony,Germany;d.8 Jan 1795-Doelzschen,Dresden,Saxony,Germany)

Missis RUEHLE(*) (b.Abt 1704-Germany)

Johann Gottlieb LIPPISCH(*) (b.15 Dec 1778-Kleinpestitz,Germany;m.28 May 1809;d.26 Aug 1841-Kleinpestitz,Germany)

A. M. NAUMANN(*) (b.Abt 1755-Germany)

Johanna F.Juliane Christiane LIPPISCH (b.6 Sep 1815-Kleinpestitz,Dresden,Saxony,Germany;d.23 Jul 1848-St. Louis,MO)

Johann Gottfried RUESTER(*) (b.Abt 1761-Germany;m.Abt 1782)

Johanna Christiana RUESTER(*) (b.16 Sep 1783-Gostritz,Saxony,Germany;d.12 Jun 1865-Kleinpestitz,Dresden,Germany)

Rosina LEUTERITZ(*) (b.Abt 1762-Germany)

Theodor Samuel KAEMPFE (b.28 Jun 1882-Frohna,Perry Co.,MO;m.8 Nov 1906;d.13 Dec 1963-Cape Girardeau,MO)

Heinrich HENNECKE (b.Abt Apr 1811-Vogelbeck,Hanover,Prussia,Germany;m.11 Oct 1846;d.8 Oct 1851-Millstadt,St. Clair Co.,IL)

Justine Engel HENNECKE (b.2 May 1847-Centreville,St. Clair Co.,IL;d.12 Sep 1925-Frohna,Perry Co.,MO)

Engell Christine Justina TUTE (b. 2 Dec 1810-Odagsen,Hanover,Germany; d.11 May 1847-Millstadt,St. Clair Co.,IL)

(*)Primary source is the Internet and is unverified.

Theodor Samuel Kaempfe
Circa 1906
He and wife Lina acquired the farm near Frohna, MO sometime after the death of his father Traugott, around 1910. Note that Theodor's name was often spelled Theodore, especially in later documents, but the earliest documents do not include the "e."

Photo courtesy of Imogene (Meyer) Unger

Chapter One

ANCIENT HISTORY AND EMIGRATION
OF
FOUR GERMAN ANCESTORS

Hennecke, Kaempfe, Lippisch, and Tute

As noted in the Introduction, four ancestors of Theodor Samuel Kaempfe came from two different regions of Germany: (1) **Duchy of Saxony**—three small towns in the area around Dresden; and (2) **Prussia**—two small towns in the Hanover province of the Kingdom of Prussia. Their dates of birth and death are incomplete but cities of origin are known. For some, enough details exist to construct a small picture of their lives, but none are as complete as for the Kaempfes.

(1) Duchy of Saxony – Kaempfe and Lippisch

The word Saxon derives from the Old German word *sahs* meaning knife or short sword. They were a warlike, piratical tribe, waging war by sending hordes of armed people in all directions. In the fifth century, the hordes invaded England so effectively that the English are still known as Anglo-Saxon. Those who remained in Europe occupied a large landmass called Saxony. Charlemagne fought for thirty years before conquering them, and that was when they became Christian. In 880, Saxony became a duchy with about 5,700 square miles of land. Various kings and nobles ruled, and borders shifted as one or the other held control. Martin Luther's reformation, as will be mentioned later in the more detailed Kaempfe emigration history, changed both the political and religious nature of Saxony, with the official state religion becoming Lutheran. In August 1813, the Saxons fought Napoleon at Dresden. They pushed him to Leipzig where a vast multi-national army defeated him and forced him to retreat beyond the Rhine.

Around that time, some of Theodor's ancestors were born near Dresden. His grandfather Johann Samuel Gottfried Kaempfe (henceforth known as Samuel Kaempfe) was probably born in Rippien (called "Rubien or Ruben by Dresden" in church records). The town was first mentioned by the name Rypin in 1296. Today it is incorporated with the city of Possendorf in the district of Bannewitz just minutes away from downtown Dresden. Agriculture, cattle and dairy production, and sandstone quarries were traditional enterprises, as depicted in their city's crest.

On February 5, 1837, Samuel Kaempfe married Johanna F. Juliana Christiane Lippisch (henceforth known as Juliane Lippisch) in Dresden, Germany, probably at St. John's Lutheran Church. They made their home in Kleinpestitz, the town from which they would emigrate when leaving Germany in 1838 with the Stephanites. The village Pestewicz was first mentioned in the year 1370, and its name, derived from its early Saxon founder, means "people plague." By 1495, the town consisted of three agricultural holdings. In 1620 a farmer named Palitzsch owned the entire complex, with twenty inhabitants.

Palitzsch Building in Kleinpestitz, Germany
Ink rendering by Carmelo L. Monti

Today, in the center of Kleinpestitz, some remarkably well-preserved historical buildings remain from those old farmsteads, dating from 1620. One, depicted on this page, is a Palitzsch building dated 1775. On a yard entry gate, a seal dating to 1777 displays a horse jumping and is now part of the municipal seal of the town. The village has been inside the city limits of Dresden since 1921.

Juliane Lippisch was born in Kleinpestitz, but earlier ancestors were born not far away in Doelzschen. The international records at www.familysearch.org list a total of seventy-one people with the last name of Lippisch. Nine were from Bohemia (now Czech Republic) or Austria, many were from Doelzschen, and one was from Rippien.

Possibly, the Lippisch family came with the Bohemian refugees of the Thirty Years War who settled near Dresden, and perhaps they were among the original Bohemian members of the St. John's parish where Martin Stephan preached. If Samuel Kaempfe knew the Lippisch family from Rippien, perhaps he traveled ten miles into Dresden to hear Stephan preach and thereby met Juliane, setting into motion their future emigration. See Chapter Two "Immigration History of Samuel Kaempfe and Juliane Lippisch" for more details.

However, a second theory could provide clues for her ancestral origins. Prior to the twelfth century, many people had only one given name. When a surname was adopted, it was often topographic, meaning it referred to their place of birth. The suffix *isch* means "of the nationality." Therefore, Lippisch means "from the country of Lippe." The historical German Principality of Lippe, dating to 1123, is located between the Weser River and the southeast part of the Teutoburg forest. Today Lippe is a part of the state of North Rhine-Westphalia in modern Germany, and its capital is Detmold, the historic capital of old Lippe. Perhaps an early male ancestor from Lippe migrated to Saxony, around the time Lippe changed from Lutheran to a form of Calvinism in 1602, and he was called, for example, Gottlieb from Lippe, or Gottlieb Lippisch. The earliest church records for the Lippisch family in Doelzschen date to 1699.

(2) Prussia – Hennecke and Tute

Two of Theodor's ancestors came from the Hanover district of Prussia: Heinrich Hennecke from Vogelbeck and his wife Engell Christine Justina Tute (henceforth known as Engell Justina Tute) from Odagsen.

By the thirteenth century, the Prussians were a Slavonic people inhabiting coastal regions surrounded by the vast plain of Northern Europe. The Poles sought to convert them to Christianity. The Teutonic knights of St. George conquered them in 1283 with that same intent and claimed the land as their own. The Poles combined forces with the Prussians to get rid of the knights, and in 1466 succeeded. West Prussia went to Poland and East Prussia became a duchy. It was in this area that nobles rose to kings, and over the next several centuries, repeatedly invaded and retreated from surrounding lands, killing over a million warriors in the process. By 1772, Prussia had become a major European power and was able to negotiate the return of much of the Polish land in West Prussia.

By 1807 Napoleon had defeated the Prussians and controlled most of the country. His armies moved east into Russia and were pushed back. By August 1813, the Saxons fought Napoleon at Dresden. They pushed him to Leipzig where a vast army that included Prussians defeated him and forced him to retreat beyond the Rhine. In 1815, Prussia was restored and became a state in the German Confederacy, ruled by Frederick Wilhelm III. In 1817, he pronounced that there would be only one Christian church in Prussia and by 1834 mandated the use of only one worship service.

The province of Hanover, which lay within the boundaries of Prussia, was originally the Duchy of Brunswick (or Braunschweig in German) home not only of several emperors and would-be emperors, but also of today's reigning British family, the Windsors. The Duchy was ruled by English royalty from 1698 to 1866 when the King of Prussia again took control. The city of Hanover is first mentioned in 1163, and it became the capital of the province in 1486. It became an important manufacturing town, and the English royalty had residences there.

About sixty miles southeast of the city of Hanover are the towns of Einbeck and Seesen. The entire area is like a living history museum set in a fairy-tale landscape of wooded mountains and wildflowers. Einbeck has its original fifteenth century walls and four hundred perfectly maintained, still-functioning Gothic and medieval half-timber houses and commercial buildings. Many have huge arch-shaped entries, designed to accommodate the enormous barrels of dark bock beer that made the town rich, as the burghers exported their product all over northern Europe.

About six miles outside Einbeck is the village of Vogelbeck. The Bird Castle (*vogel* means bird in German) is the earthen remains of a pre-historic fortress dating to 400 B.C. Evidence suggests that portions were rebuilt in the Middle Ages, but that too is gone. Other Iron Age settlement remains have been found in the area, suggesting a fairly large population surrounded the castle. Two Roman coins have been found in archaeological excavations, dating to 12 A.D. An amber bead believed to be 4,000 years old was also unearthed. Origins of the modern town date to 1184 with a monastery. The French controlled the town from 1807 to 1813, when Napoleon was beaten at Leipzig.

Until 1850, Vogelbeck was a tiny agricultural community. The main road went around the town, and the only water was from wells. After that, roads and water became more accessible, and the town grew. Potash for cement was mined, so many landowners prospered from the royalties. A new cement plant provided new jobs, so the population doubled from 1825 to 1925. The church was built in 1913 to replace an old chapel. The town has suffered several floods, fires, and ravages of war, so it is not as well preserved as nearby Einbeck.

Justine Engel (Hennecke) Kaempfe's parents both came from this area. Church records for Trinity Lutheran Church in Millstadt, Illinois show that Heinrich Hennecke was born in "Vogelbeck Koenigreich (Kingdom) Hanover" about April 1811. Church records for Zion Evangelical Church in Millstadt show that Engell Justina Tute was born in Odagsen, Hanover, Germany, which is located about three miles west of Vogelbeck and four miles south of Einbeck, on December 2, 1810. Online resources show two Heinrich Henneckes born in Vogelbeck, in 1746 and 1770, father and son. However, at this time, there is no evidence to link them to the Heinrich Hennecke born about 1811. If the link is ever made, then those additional records link to a maternal line that goes back four more generations to 1600. Furthermore, another family headed by Christiane Hennecke (born about 1812) emigrated from Volgelbeck, Germany to "the State of Illinois" in 1852, a year after Heinrich's death, and a five-year-old son in that family was named Heinrich, suggesting a familial link between the two men.

An Illinois marriage license shows that Henreich (*sic*) Hennecke married Justina Tute on October 11, 1846. He was thirty-five and she was thirty-six. No place of birth is provided on that document, but in the 1920 U.S. census Justine (Hennecke) Kaempfe stated that both of her parents were from Hanover. Therefore, the evidence shows that Heinrich and Engell Justina were both born in Prussia and immigrated to Millstadt before 1846 as single people. Not known is why they came or if they came with their parents, but given Fredrick Wilhelm III's mandate for one church, religious freedom was likely a contributing factor.

At first glance, the ethnicity of Theodor Samuel Kaempfe and his father Traugott appears simply to be German. A closer study reveals a much greater diversity, and likely includes Bohemian, Saxon, Slavonic, and Thuringian lines. Milda (Kaempfe) Monti once stated that her father Theodor believed that the Lippisch line might be Jewish, which corresponds to a Bohemian background. These ancestors were probably all freemen (landholders) or freedmen (non-landholders but free to farm), given their ability to leave Germany and their apparent financial resources to do so.

CHAPTER TWO

IMMIGRATION HISTORY
OF
SAMUEL KAEMPFE AND JULIANE LIPPISCH

Samuel Kaempfe, his wife Juliane Lippisch, and their first-born son Samuel, who all emigrated with a group of religious zealots called the Stephanites, are of particular interest because of the great amount of information available in Walter O. Forster's book *Zion on the Mississippi*. A study of what led to their exodus—religious persecution, differences in church doctrine of the many newly formed protestant faiths, and the power of a charismatic church leader—sheds light on both their lives and on the lives and histories of other German ancestors.

After Martin Luther died in 1546, theological debate continued for decades until the publication of "Book of Concord" in 1580, now known as the Lutheran Confessions. Because the church lacked good leaders and controversy over interpretation continued, the heads of various German states took control. By the late 1600's corruption compromised church leadership and the influence of Rationalism reached deeply into the theological realm of thinking. Reason and science as the basis for morality began to replace faith in the un-provable lessons of the Bible. The Pietists reacted by pursuing more in-depth Bible study, pious living to serve as an example, and mission service, emphasizing deeds over creed. Newer protestant, reformed churches rejected Luther and followed ideas of John Calvin. During the Thirty Years War protestant fugitives left Bohemia (Czech Republic) and moved to Saxony. By 1650 St. John's Church

St. John's Church in Dresden, Germany
Destroyed in World War Two
Illustration courtesy of Concordia Historical Institute

in Dresden was assigned to them, and they were permitted variations in their services and church organization not permitted elsewhere. In 1810, the congregation exercised its unique freedom to choose their pastor when they called the controversial Martin Stephan, a powerful, charismatic Pietist-leaning Lutheran, who had never graduated from the University of Leipzig. The congregation consisted of thirty families in 1810, but by 1819, it had grown to over a thousand members as Stephan's admirers traveled from other parishes to hear him speak.

Communion Chalice
Trinity Lutheran Church

Made of silver, gold and painted porcelain in Austria for a monastery in Spain, it was "acquired" by a Saxon prince during the Napoleonic Wars, and he gave it to the Stephanites when they left Germany in 1838. Samuel and Juliane Kaempfe probably took Communion from this chalice aboard the *Johann Georg* or in St. Louis, Missouri, at the original Trinity Lutheran Church.

Photo by Carmelo L. Monti

Speculatively, the Lippisch family was one of the thirty families, and Samuel Kaempfe was one of the admirers who traveled to hear him.

By the 1800's various regional governments dictated church doctrine and limited how Lutherans could worship. Rationalism and Pietism competed for supremacy and the souls of the Lutherans. In 1817, King Fredrick Wilhelm III of Prussian dictated that there would be only one Christian church in Prussia and by 1834, mandated one style of worship service. His theology denied the real presence of Christ's body and blood in the Lord's Supper and disputed Baptism as a means of grace.

In Saxony, things were not much different, and the conservative element among the Lutherans pointed to Prussia as an example of what was to come. As tough as things had been for decades, emigration for Stephan did not become essential until his personal difficulties pushed him in that direction. His parishioners maintained a cottage in the forest for him, and an elite clique held frequent late night meetings there; he was known to solicit gifts from his followers; he spent little time at home with his wife and ten children and was even accused of immorality with a female servant. In 1836, Stephan was arrested and many of his followers were subjected to scrutiny. They were forbidden to hold nighttime meetings. Although never convicted of any criminal charge and released, he was pillared by the press; he asserted that he and his group were being persecuted after he was suspended from his office in the official church.

Discussion of emigration came and went until December 1837, when Stephan set up a committee to begin the planning. His personal reasons were never discussed openly, and long documents were written to establish the basis for their leaving and establishment of a new church. The concept that they were "The Church" and that emigration meant the difference between damnation and salvation was put forth. Stephan held ultimate authority over all decisions. They would travel to Bremen and take chartered ships to New Orleans, Louisiana, then travel by steamboat to St. Louis, Missouri. They would stay temporarily in St. Louis while a permanent location was found. They would take along all necessary accoutrements for their religious services, including altar vessels and sacrificial wine. A common treasury would be established to finance the emigration, purchase supplies for the trip, buy land in Missouri, and finance the administration of the enterprise. Wealthier followers would contribute the funds, and loans would be extended to a few indigent but worthy emigrants. As profits accrued from their enterprises in their new home, the original investors would be repaid. Their intention was to form a semiautonomous theocratic community, with power held largely by the clergy, and secondly by a privileged wealthy group of investors. They accumulated between $55,000 and $80,604 in their communal fund. Thus began the Emigration Association, later known as the Gesellschaft.

By July 1838, the group had signed a contract to charter its first ship, the *Olbers*. News of the group's emigration plans spread across Saxony, generating that era's equivalent of our modern media frenzy. Such a singular mass-exodus was unheard of in Saxony. Newspaper articles, editorials, cartoons, all served to increase interest, and soon the group's numbers swelled from two hundred to nearly seven hundred. Stephan was placed under house arrest, while others on the committee went and chartered more ships. Letters from all over Saxony poured in with applications for inclusion. Sixty-eight percent of the personal

Three-Masted Ship the *Olbers*
The Gesellschaft traveled from Germany to America in 1838 aboard the *Olbers*. Samuel Kaempfe and his family traveled aboard a similar three-masted ship, the *Johann Georg*.
Illustration courtesy of Concordia Historical Institute

accounts in the Gesellschaft showed a deficit. Eventually many would admit that their true motivation for leaving Saxony was more economic than religious, but for others the move meant breaking ties with family members who did not hold their religious beliefs.

In 1838, six hundred sixty-five followers boarded five three-masted sailing ships in Bremerhaven. Martin Stephan was aboard the *Olbers*, and he left behind his wife and nine of his ten children, taking only his oldest son. Onboard the *Johann Georg* was Samuel Kaempfe and his family; Gottlieb Palisch with his wife Christiana (Kaempfe) Palisch, who is believed to be an older sister to Samuel; and Gottlieb Palitzsch also from Kleinpestitz. The *Johann Georg* was the second ship to leave on November 3, 1838, and took sixty-four days to cross the stormy Atlantic, arriving in New Orleans on January 5, 1839.

The *Amalia* left port last on November 18 with fifty-three of the followers, and was never seen again, lost at sea during a month of continuous storms that the other ships had encountered. This was devastating to the group, not only for the loss of life, but also because this particular ship carried many of their supplies and a great amount of cash.

While at sea, the members voted to confer upon Stephan the title of Herr Bishop and signed a Pledge of Subjugation to him. The hierarchy of clergy wrote codes that defined a theocracy. As each ship arrived in New Orleans, the groups secured passage onboard steamships for transportation to St. Louis where they planned to meet. The *Johann Georg* group left on January 12 aboard the *Clyde* and arrived on January 24, 1839. St. Louis offered employment but not the warmest welcome from earlier German immigrants. Many of them were of the Rational persuasion, and they viewed the newly arrived Gesellschaft members as dupes and slaves to a clergy that was either corrupt or mentally ill.

The economic realities of their venture took their toll immediately. Cost of steamship travel exceeded original estimates, exacerbated by luxurious food and wine for Stephan's inner circle. Rent in St. Louis was higher than expected which left only five-cents a day per person for food and little for wood to make fires. Stephan demanded an apartment suitable to a Bishop and a new carriage, declaring that the old one transported from Germany was unsuitable for St. Louis. Stephan took more money for his personal use than he put into the fund before leaving Germany, and that pattern escalated after they arrived in St. Louis. Eventually, it would contribute to his undoing.

St. Louis was a harsh place to live. The death rate in St. Louis was one in twenty-three for adults but 40% for children under age five. The unpaved streets were quagmires of garbage and pig and horse feces, breeding grounds for frequent outbreaks of cholera, influenza, and smallpox. About seventy members of the Gesellschaft died within four months of arriving in St. Louis. As such, the acquisition of land should have been their first priority, but weeks slipped by before the effort began, as they wasted time ordering new clerical robes and church regalia lost on the *Amalia*.

Although government-owned land in the recently formed states of Illinois and Missouri was available at $1.25 an acre, many sites were rejected. Instead, they used $8,234 (or $9,234 depending on source) to purchase 4,475 acres of privately owned and government land in the Perry County area, with an average price of $2.06 per acre. J.G. Gube made the purchases with cash and registered the land in his name. Much of the land was of medium quality for farming, and some was very poor and swamp-like. Only a few buildings existed but they did have a Mississippi River landing. Nearby Tower Rock has been called their "Plymouth Rock."

Stephan and the hardiest men, mostly farmers, left St. Louis to establish the communities of Altenburg, Wittenberg, Nieder-Frohna (*sic*), Dresden, and Seelitz in Perry County, and Johannesburg in Cape Girardeau County in 1839. Paitzdorf (later known as Uniontown) was established in 1840. While Stephan occupied the farmhouse, the others suffered deplorable conditions as they built roads and bridges instead of more houses, at Stephan's insistence. In

Johann Samuel Gottfried Kaempfe
Circa 1876—Notice the diamond stickpin in his necktie

Photo courtesy of Milda (Kaempfe) Monti Estate

leaving behind most of his inner circle of clergy and administrators, Stephan unwittingly set in motion his own demise. By then, most of them had come to despise his leadership, and his absence gave them the opportunity to ferment a rebellion. When three women came forward to confess sexual misconduct with Stephan in May 1839, his fate was sealed.

Eventually, in addition to sexual misconduct, Stephan was blamed for the financially ruined Gesellschaft because he took along too many poor people, he made too many unnecessary expenditures, he wasted precious time in St. Louis, and he approved a poor choice of location bought with cash instead of credit. His fellow clergy decided within a week to excommunicate him, and they sent C.F.W. Walther to Perry County to persuade the lay leaders that this was necessary. Stephan was to be banished from the colony and warned to never to return to Missouri. The lay leaders resisted, but by May 19, the whole colony was buzzing with gossip and outrage. That Sunday, Stephan ordered everyone to come to Wittenberg to hear his sermon, while Walther summoned everyone to Altenburg. Everyone ignored Stephan and went to Altenburg.

By May 30, an angry mob turned Stephan out of his house, and he was rowed across the Mississippi with a few personal possessions and $100 and left on the riverbank. Sixteen days later, his housemaid, one of those who had confessed her relationship with Stephan, escaped the colony and joined him in Illinois. By 1841, his son Martin Stephan Jr., the only family member to accompany him to America, abandoned the cause and returned to Saxony.

Between one and two hundred of the followers, mostly craftsmen who could find no work in Perry County, were instructed to stay in St. Louis, but the others resolved to move to Perry County, where they spread out among the various newly established communities. Their life was intolerable. The lay leaders, with new found power, and the clergy, who filled the vacuum left by Stephan, moved their families into the few newly built houses and argued over which group would now govern the community. Most of the people, including men, women and children, slept in lean-tos, shacks, or even out in the open, they and their baggage getting drenched in the spring rains. By summer, the Gesellschaft was depleted of funds. They would have starved but for the generosity of earlier settlers—the English, Scotch, Irish and French. Without enough draught animals, they labored manually, clearing land and moving logs for cabins. The death rate from various fevers soared. Women gave birth without benefit of midwives, so there was a high mortality rate for both mother and child. Bitterness, envy, and dissension over how the colony would be governed without Herr Bishop raged for the next two years. Some of the emigrants gave up and left.

In August 1839, the man who held title to all the land, J. G. Gube, died. Under Missouri law, his estate went into probate court. Thirty-nine of the original investors to the Gesellschaft filed a petition in November, claiming the land should be divided between them. Among the signers were Samuel Kaempfe, Gottlieb Palisch and Gottlieb Palitzsch. The petitioners provided the court with a map that illustrated the division of land. Samuel Kaempfe, a farmer, was given a lot that measured one-sixteenth of a section near the community of Dresden, because he had emigrated from Kleinpestitz near the city of Dresden in Germany. He was joint owner of two smaller lots, also near Dresden, with Gottlieb Palisch, likely his brother-in-law. Those two smaller lots were donated to the community so that both a public school and a parochial school could be built. No doubt, Samuel began building a house and farming his land. (See USGS Map Altenburg Quadrangle on page 26 for location of the lots.)

On August 10, 1840, Traugott Kaempfe was born in Altenburg, the second son of Samuel and Juliane Kaempfe. On July 15, 1842, twin sons Carl and Ernst were born. Ernst died immediately and was buried at Trinity Lutheran Church in Altenburg. On August 30, 1842, a friend Christoph Paul died of fever in their home. The evidence shows that the family had been in Perry County during much of this difficult era.

The Great Flood of 1844 may have influenced many former Gesellschaft members to move. It remains the biggest on record with a discharge of 1,300,000 cubic feet per second at St. Louis. Recent history shows that the Great Flood of 1993 took many months to grow from minor flooding to the monster it became, so in 1844 flooding likely occurred over a similar slow-motion timetable. The devastation was so widespread that Congress passed the Swamp Act in 1849 for the purpose of building levees.

In 1844, Martin Stephan disappeared from Kaskaskia records and first appeared in Red Bud records, suggesting the flood influenced him. That year he organized a congregation at Horse Prairie where he preached until his death on February 22, 1846. No evidence exists to show that any former Gesellschaft members resumed a cordial relationship with him. He's buried at Trinity Lutheran Church in Red Bud, Illinois. Eventually, C. F. W. Walther, not Stephan, would be known as the founding father of the Lutheran Church Missouri Synod.

Likewise, on April 26, 1844, Samuel and Juliane Kaempfe's young son Carl died in St. Louis and was buried in the old Trinity Cemetery at Ohio and Miami Streets. The family apparently moved, as evidenced by Samuel Kaempfe's listing as a member of Trinity Lutheran Church in Millstadt, Illinois, beginning in 1844. Exactly when they left for Millstadt is not clear, but other members of the emigration group who had sufficient funds sought escape from the difficult life and high death rate—and no doubt the floods—in Perry County by moving to Illinois and purchasing land there. Therefore, Samuel Kaempfe, despite devastating losses with the Gesellschaft investment, still had enough funds to leave Altenburg in the early-1840s and escape to the richer soil of Illinois.

However, in regards to the death toll, life was no kinder there. Trinity Lutheran Church in St. Louis (see Chalice on page 12) recorded that three more children died as infants or toddlers between 1847 and 1848 and they were buried in the old Trinity Cemetery. Their mother Juliane (Lippisch) Kaempfe also died July 23, 1848 of lung disease in St. Louis, as recorded in church records, but her place of burial is unknown. So by the end of 1848, Samuel had buried his wife and five children but still had two living sons, Traugott age eight and Samuel age ten years old. On January 1, 1850, he married a second time, to a widow, Christiane (Mueller) Moos with three children. Between 1851 and 1860 they had five children together, but only three lived long enough to reach adulthood and marry. Those three were half-siblings to Traugott Kaempfe, and one lived long enough to become one of the aunts from Illinois that Milda (Kaempfe) Monti remembered from her childhood.

The 1860 U.S. Census for Illinois, St. Clair County, Millstadt Post Office, shows Sam Kaempfe (age 48) working as a farmer, with $4000 in real estate, born in Saxony. Other household members included Christiane (41) born in Nassau, Germany; Sam'l (21) born in Saxony; Traugott (20) born in Missouri; Fred Mos (*sic*) (18) and Mimma Mos (*sic*)(17) both born in Nassau; Gottfried (7), Wm. (9), Magdalena (6), and Christiana Kaempfe (3) all born in Illinois.

In March 1865, Samuel and Juliane's oldest son Samuel, who had been aboard the *Johann Georg*, died in the Civil War without having married. See Chapter Three "Killed in the Civil War" for more details. In 1866 Samuel and Christiane became members of the Holy Cross Lutheran Church. Christiane died in 1875. In 1876 Juliane's then oldest living son Traugott took his entire family and moved to Frohna, Perry County, Missouri. Some researchers thought that he returned to the area to farm Samuel's Gesellschaft land, but that assertion was proved wrong when Imogene (Meyer) Unger determined that Traugott purchased a different farm, west of Frohna, on December 7, 1876 from Robert M. Smith and wife. Exactly when Samuel sold his Missouri Gesellschaft land has not been determined.

Samuel Kaempfe died in 1879 and to date his place of death and burial are unknown. Cindy (Bachmann) Brigham thinks he is buried in Holy Cross—Kleinschmidt Cemetery, Sugar Loaf Township, Millstadt, Illinois, but she stated his headstone has never been found. In a visit to the cemetery in 2003, this author found numerous Kaempfe headstones, including one that reads "Juliane Drewes, 21 Jun 1851, 18 Mar 1880." To the left of her headstone is an open gravesite with no stone. To the left of that open site is a headstone for "Wilhelm L. Kaempfe, 18 Mar 1851, 30 Jan 1878." Then to the left of that stone is "Christiana (unreadable) Samuel G. Kempfe, Geboren Mueller, 21 March 1819, 3 Feb 1875." Since Samuel Kaempfe died in 1879, he is likely buried in the open gravesite with no stone. His second wife Christiana (Mueller) died first in 1875; then his son Wilhelm died in 1878; then Samuel died in 1879; and finally, Juliane (Hofstetter) Kaempfe-Drewes died in 1880. They were buried consecutively. Having been married less than a year, Juliane's second husband Louis Drewes likely would have buried her next to her first husband Wilhelm Kaempfe, but if that open site was occupied, he could only place her next in line. Logic dictates that Samuel is buried here, between Juliane and Wilhelm.

Holy Cross - Kleinschimdt Cemetery
Millstadt, Illinois
Above: Christiana (Mueller) Moos-Kaempfe
Right: Juliane (Hofstetter) Kaempfe-Drewes
Left: Wilhelm L. Kaempfe
Samuel Gottfried Kaempfe is likely buried in an unmarked grave between Juliane and Wilhelm.
Photos by Carmelo L. Monti

Map of Illinois and Missouri
Showing locations of Millstadt, Illinois and St. Louis, Cape Girardeau and Perry Counties in Missouri
Map drawn by Carmelo L. Monti

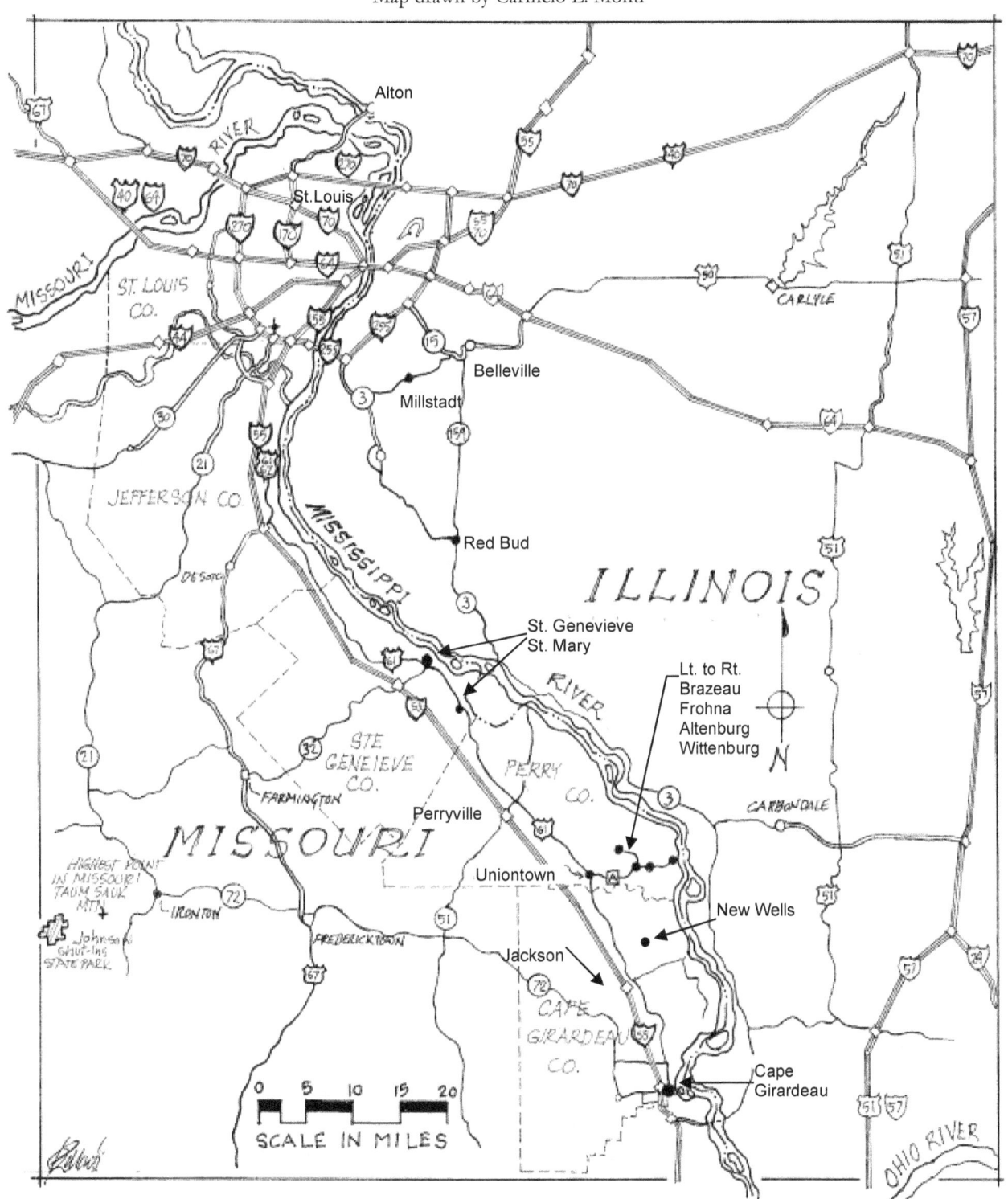

No. 2.

RECORD OF DEATH AND INTERMENT.

Name and number of person interred.	*Samuel Kaempfe* *562*
Number and locality of the grave . .	*1 Row 1 Ill Sol New Ce—*
Hospital number of the deceased . .	*6217*
Regiment, rank, and company . . .	*20th Ill Vol* *Private Wnd*
Residence before enlistment . . .	*St. Clair Co Ill*
Conjugal condition, (and if married, the residence of the widow) . .	*Single*
Cause of death	*Gun Shot Wound Chest, penetrating the Lungs*
Age of the deceased	*26 Years*
Nativity	*Germany*
References and remarks	*Admitted March 10th 1865,*
Date of death and burial	*5 P.M. March 15th 2.30 P.M March 1865 .*

[A duplicate of this Record has been forwarded to the Sexton, and another remains at this Hospital.]

To *Brig Genl L. Thomas*
    Adjt Genl U S A

SIR:

It becomes my duty to inform you that the person above described died at this Hospital as herein stated ; and that it is desired his remains should be interred with the usual military honors.

Respectfully,

C. Hovgill Wm
Surgeon U. S. Army.
in Charge

MILITARY HOSPITAL, *Foster New Berne N.C.*

This copy of Record is to be transmitted to the Adjutant General at Washington immediately after the place of burial and the number of the grave have been ascertained and registered. The above notification is to remain attached.

Record of Death and Interment
for Samuel Kaempfe Jr.

Official copy provided by the National Archives and Records Administration, Washington DC

CHAPTER THREE

KILLED IN THE CIVIL WAR: SAMUEL KAEMPFE JR.

Johann Samuel Gottfried Kaempfe (henceforth known as Samuel Kaempfe Jr.) was born in Germany on June 4, 1838; emigrated to the U.S. with his parents in 1839; and was only twenty-six years old in 1864 when active recruiting of enlistees for the Union took place in St. Clair County, Illinois. In fact, about 4,400 from St. Clair served in the Union at one time or another. They were organized into various regiments and sent off to fight wherever needed. Most served a three-year stint, concentrating in Tennessee, and then moving into Georgia, South Carolina, and North Carolina.

The Military Records for Samuel Kaempfe Jr. provide a lot of information about him and his short, tragic military career. A single man, he stood five-feet six-inches tall and had gray eyes and brown hair. Coming from a farming family in St. Clair County, Illinois and working as a laborer in Alton most likely produced his dark complexion. On September 21, 1864, he either enlisted or was drafted into the Union Army. By October he was a Private located in Joliet,

Wool Marker Flag
(17 in. X 22 in.) flown by the 132nd Regiment New York Infantry in the Civil War. Samuel Kaempfe Jr. was serving under this flag on temporary duty with them when he was killed in 1865.
Photo courtesy of New York State Division of Military & Naval Affairs and NY National Guard

Illinois, assigned to Milliken's New Company with Company E, 20th Regiment Illinois Infantry. In November he was in Chattanooga, Tennessee and was admitted to the hospital there for almost a whole month.

In January 1865, he was temporarily attached to the 132nd New York Infantry. Around that time, General Sherman torched Atlanta and went through Savanna. His troops burned Columbia, South Carolina in February 1865. Union forces had a stronghold at New Berne, North Carolina, which they had captured in 1862 and had held during the entire war. The Battle of Wyse Fork involved Union troops stationed at New Berne who left there to go capture Goldsboro. A battle took place March 7 to 10, 1865, which resulted in 1,101 Union casualties. Young Samuel Kaempfe Jr. was one of them.

On March 8, Samuel was fighting at Wises (*sic*) Cross Roads, N.C. with the 132nd when he received a gunshot wound to his chest that penetrated his lungs. Two days later he was admitted to Foster General Hospital and he suffered five days before he died on March 15, at 2:30 in the afternoon. He was buried the next day in the clothes he was wearing in the New Bern National Cemetery in New Berne, North Carolina, with the usual military honors. His grave is unmarked and has not been found. His great-grand-nephew Courtney Meyer visited the Cemetery, inquired about the grave, and was told that many graves were never marked. Samuel's Military Records kept by the National Archives include five Muster cards with descriptive information about him while in the 20th Regiment Illinois Infantry, Company E (Union); two pages of hospital records; one card for Inventory of the Effects; two pages for Record of Death and Interment; and three cards with Notations for the Adjutant General's Office. He had never been paid but had an outstanding debt for the cost of his uniform for $39.31. A final accounting shows a figure of $4.35 but does not make clear if this was paid to his estate or if it was owed by him. He had served his country less than six months, was wounded twice, and died fighting, and, sadly, the last thing known of him is that final accounting.

All records clustered together in his file folder have various spellings of his last name. The book "Roll of Honor-Vol. 10" published in 1866 lists Samuel Kamper (*sic*) in the 20th Regiment, his date of death March. 16, 1865, and his burial in New Bern National Cemetery, NC. The church records for Holy Cross Lutheran Church in St. Clair County, Millstadt, Illinois, page 49, describes Samuel Gottfr. KAEMPFE / KEMPF, born June 4, 1838, in Dresden, Germany, and died March 15, 1865, in New Bern, N.C. Therefore, despite the variations in the spelling of his name and errors in the dates, there is no doubt that they are one and the same person, Samuel Gottfried Kaempfe Jr.

Slavery

One part of the eight ancestors' history in Missouri has not been addressed: slave ownership. Missouri was a slave state, and many people in Perry and Cape Girardeau County did own slaves prior to the Civil War. However, most German Lutherans did not because they were opposed to it on principal, and there is no evidence to suggest that any of the eight ancestors, who immigrated between 1839 and 1855, did so.

Illinois was a free state, and, as mentioned, Samuel Kaempfe Jr., who immigrated as a baby, died fighting for the Union. In addition, the Civil War website has numerous listings for Koenigs, Henneckes, and Tutes who also fought on the side of the Union, but no evidence has been found to link them directly to the eight ancestors. Should new data materialize, more research could be done in this area.

Chapter Four

POST-IMMIGRATION HISTORY FOR ONE GERMAN LINE

Hennecke/Tute and Kaempfe/Hennecke

The post-immigration history of Engell Justina Tute and Heinrich Hennecke is nearly as complete as that of Kaempfe/Lippisch, but not as detailed. Census records have been viewed; church records exist for some of them; but no books have been written which specifically include them. Many of these details along with oral history have come together to create an interesting, albeit, limited picture. In their emigration history, this couple arrived sometime prior to 1846, perhaps as children with parents, in Millstadt, Illinois, from Vogelbeck and Odagsen in the Hanover province of Prussia, but the dates of their journeys have not been found. Church records show two other Hennecke families, headed by August Conrad and Johann Wilhelm Hennecke, who also emigrated from Vogelbeck to Millstadt around the same time, but it is unknown if they were related to Heinrich or if they left descendants. Furthermore, another family headed by Christiane Hennecke (born about 1812) emigrated from Volgelbeck, Germany to "the State of Illinois" in 1852, a year after Heinrich's death, and a five-year-old son in that family was named Heinrich, suggesting a familial link between the two men.

An Illinois marriage license shows that Henreich (*sic*) Hennecke married Justine Tute on October 11, 1846. Heinrich's trade was master mason. On May 2, 1847, their first and only child Justine Engel Hennecke was born. Nine days later on May 11, 1847 Engell Justina died, likely from complications during the birth of her daughter. She was thirty-seven years old and was buried in Zion Evangelical Church's Frievogel Cemetery in Millstadt with no headstone.

On October 29, 1848, Heinrich remarried to Maria Elisabeth (Lutz). The first child of that union was born on February 20, 1850. A second child had already been conceived when Heinrich Hennecke died on October 8, 1851 at age "forty years and six months" from "nervenfieber," leaving Maria a widow with her step-child Justine, her infant son and another child on the way. A baby girl was born on February 2, 1852, and on May 31, 1852, she remarried to Friedrich Buchholz. Therefore, by age five, Justine Engel Hennecke had lost both natural parents and was being raised by two stepparents, with both half-siblings and stepsiblings in the household. Maria and Friedrich produced three more children. In 1870 Justine's stepmother died, and her stepfather Buchholz remarried the same year to Anna Christine Amalie Sauthof, who was also a widow with one child. They apparently had no new children together.

Justine left her large stepfamily when she married Traugott Kaempfe on May 7, 1865, but the couple remained in Illinois for eleven years. Finally, Traugott and Justine (Hennecke) Kaempfe left Millstadt in 1876 and moved to Perry County, Missouri, where he had been born, and they purchased a farm west of Frohna from Robert M. Smith on December 7, 1876.

Concordia Lutheran Church
Frohna, Perry County, Missouri
Photo by Mary L. Miller

Milda (Kaempfe) Monti recalled having "aunts from Illinois," but was uncertain of how they were related. Justine left behind one surviving half-sibling, Wilhelmine August Louise (Hennecke) Preusser, who produced seven children. Dates of death for the Preusser family are unknown, so it's unclear if they knew Milda. Traugott left behind three half-siblings, but only two lived long enough to have known Milda. They were Marie Magdalene (Kaempfe) Hofstetter who died in 1932 and Johann Gottfried Kaempfe who died in 1938. Collectively, they produced ten children who also lived long enough to have known Milda.

Traugott and Justine produced eight children. Five were born in Illinois and three in Missouri after their move to Perry County. They grew up on the farm, but as adults some of them left the area, moving to cities or even other states. Louise, their oldest daughter, married Claus Stueve but the couple never had children. She received internal injuries during the Great Tornado and died ten days later in 1925. Another daughter Charlotte married Joseph Stueve (or Stuive) and moved to Sylvan Grove, Kansas around 1903 where they had at least three children. Traugott's third daughter Anna married Otto Oswald and they had five children, all born in Frohna. Four survived to adulthood. Anna and Otto later moved to Madison, Nebraska, about one hundred-twenty miles northwest of Omaha, and some of their children remained there. One of Anna's sons moved to Kansas and has descendants there. Otto Oswald died in 1941 and is buried in Frohna, but Anna died in Nebraska in 1954.

Traugott and Justine's oldest son Wilhelm "William" married Anna Mangels and they had at least four children. They were living in Menfro, MO where he was a farmer when he died from "hemorrhage" at age forty-five in 1922. Another son Otto married Magdalena Mueller and they had six children, but she hanged herself six weeks after their last son was born in 1911. Otto then married Martha Gemeinhardt, but he died from pneumonia in 1916. Martha and her stepchildren moved in with her sister-in-law Louise (Kaempfe) Stueve. Martha was killed instantly during the Great Tornado, and as noted above, Louise died ten days later from her injuries. Another son Carl "Charles" married Frieda Burfeind and they had nine children. He moved to Cape Girardeau where he worked as a fireman in a shoe factory until he died in 1946 from cancer. Another son Heinrich Ernst never married and died in 1952 from prostate cancer.

Finally, their youngest son Theodor Kaempfe married Lina Koenig, bought Traugott's farm where he had been reared, and raised his family of six there. See Chapter Eleven "Growing Up on a Farm Near Frohna" and Chapter Twelve "Portraits of Eight Kaempfe Siblings" for more details about his expansion of the farm and the lives of his children. When Traugott died on December 11, 1909, his death was recorded at Concordia Lutheran Church, but Perry County did not issue official death certificates prior to 1910, so cause of death is not known.

His wife Justine lived to be seventy-eight years old when she died from paralysis on September 12, 1925. Her son Theodore (*sic*) gave the information for her death certificate, and his spelling for her parents' names (Wm. Henneke and Christina Tuede, both from Germany) differs from the 1846 Illinois marriage license for her parents (Henreich Hennecke and Justine Tute) noted above, presenting yet another flawed document to interpret in the genealogical quest for accuracy. Traugott and Justine were both buried in Concordia Cemetery at Concordia Lutheran Church in Frohna.

The Family of Traugott Gotthilf and Justine Engel (Hennecke) Kaempfe
Circa 1900
Justine and Traugott are seated. Children, standing, from left to right:
Carl, Charlotte, Ernst, Otto, Anna, William, Louise, and Theodor
Photo courtesy of Milda (Kaempfe) Monti Estate

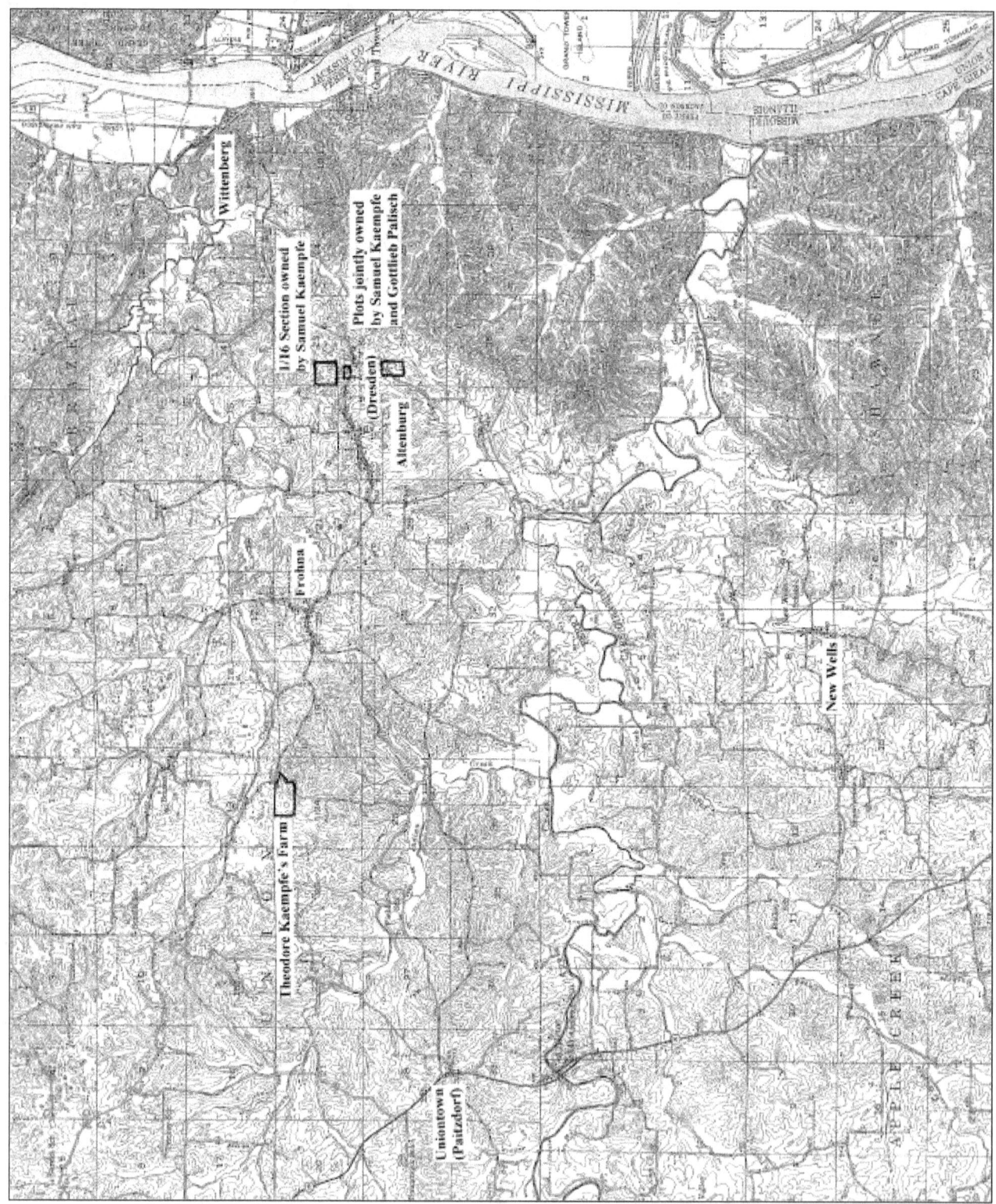

U.S.G.S. Map Altenburg Quadrangle, MO-ILL 1949
Kaempfe Farms near Frohna and Altenburg, Perry County, Missouri
Map created by Mary L. Miller

Traugott Gotthilf Kaempfe
Circa 1895
Photo courtesy of Milda (Kaempfe) Monti Estate

Kaempfe Woman
Justine Engel (Hennecke) Kaempfe (right) with two unknown Kaempfe women

Sheep on the Farm

Photos courtesy of Imogene (Meyer) Unger

CHAPTER FIVE

DESCENDANTS OF HEINRICH HENNECKE AND ADAM LIPPISCH

Descendants of Heinrich HENNECKE

1. Heinrich HENNECKE (b.Abt Apr 1811-Vogelbeck,Hanover,Prussia,Germany;d.8 Oct 1851-Millstadt,IL)
- sp: Engell Christine Justina TUTE (b. 2 Dec 1810-Odagsen, Hanover,Ger.;m.11 Oct 1846;d.11 May 1847-Millstadt,IL)
  - 2. Justine Engel HENNECKE (b.2 May 1847-Centreville,St. Clair Co.,IL;d.12 Sep 1925-Frohna,Perry Co.,MO)
    - sp: Traugott Gotthilf KAEMPFE (b.10 Aug 1840-Altenburg,Perry Co.,MO;m.7 May 1865;d.11 Dec 1909-Frohna,MO)

For Descendants of Justine Engel Hennecke and Traugott Gotthilf Kaempfe see Chapter Six

- sp: Maria Elisabethe LUTZ (b.30 Mar 1817-Altweilnau Herzog,Germany;m.29 Oct 1848;d.21 Jan 1870-Millstadt,IL)
  - 2. Johann Peter Wilhelm HENNECKE (b.20 Feb 1850-Millstadt,IL;d.20 Sep 1867-Millstadt,St. Clair Co.,IL)
  - 2. Wilhelmine Auguste Louise HENNECKE (b.2 Feb 1852-Millstadt,St. Clair Co.,IL)
    - sp: Peter Wilhelm PREUSSER (b.8 Jun 1849-Centreville Twp.,St. Clair Co.,IL;m.31 Jul 1870)
      - 3. Amalie Katherina PREUSSER (b.14 Sep 1871-IL)
      - 3. Johann Friedrich Wilhelm PREUSSER (b.29 Apr 1874-IL)
      - 3. Elisabethe Augusta PREUSSER (b.10 Oct 1876-IL)
      - 3. Carl Gottlieb PREUSSER (b.26 Jan 1879-Illinois;d.1 Dec 1882-Millstadt,St. Clair Co.,IL)
      - 3. Eduard Heinrich G. PREUSSER (b.21 May 1881-IL)
      - 3. Louise Wilhelmine PREUSSER (b.5 Dec 1883-IL;d.8 Aug 1884-Millstadt,St. Clair Co.,IL)
      - 3. Anna Marie Louise PREUSSER (b.7 Aug 1885-IL)

Note : Heinrich Hennecke died on Oct. 8, 1851 while his second wife Marie Elisabeth Lutz was pregnant with their second child. The widow Marie, who already had a step-daughter Justine Engel Hennecke and her first son Johann Peter, married Johann Friederick Gerhard Buckholz on May 31, 1852 just three months after the birth of her daughter Wilhelmine. They went on to have three children:

> Wilh. Christian Gottfried BUCKHOLZ (b. 24 Oct. 1854-Millstadt, St. Clair Co., IL; d. 2 Sep. 1856)
>
> Henrietta Friederike Caroline BUCKHOLZ (b. 13 Feb. 1858-Millstadt, St. Clair Co.,IL; d. 25 Apr. 1884)
>
> Elisabeth Theresse BUCKHOLZ (b. 10 Feb. 1861-Millstadt, St. Clair Co., IL; d. 3 Mar. 1890)

Thus Justine Engel Hennecke, at age five in 1852, having lost both of her natural parents, was raised by two stepparents in a household with half-siblings and stepsiblings. She married Traugott Kaempfe on May 7, 1865. On Jan. 21, 1870 Marie died, leaving Buckholz with one stepchild (Wilhelmine Auguste Louise Hennecke) and two of his own children (his son had already died). Buckholz then married a widow Anna Christine Amalie Sautauf on July 18, 1870. She brought one child Georg A. Sautauf to their marriage, but they apparently had no children together.

Descendants of Adam LIPPISCH (*)

1. Adam LIPPISCH(*) (b.1699-Doelzschen,Dresden,Saxony,Germany;d.31 Mar 1762)

   sp: Martha UNKNOWN(*) (b.5 Aug 1701-Doelzschen,Dresden,Saxony,Germany;m.Abt 1725;d.15 Oct 1758)

    2. Johann George LIPPISCH(*) (b.22 Sep 1726-Doelzschen,Germany;d.31 Mar 1760-Doelzschen,,Germany)

     sp: Maria RUEHLE(*) (b.1726-Gostritz,Saxony,Germany;m.23 Apr 1749;d.8 Jan 1795-Doelzschen,Germany)

     3. Johann Gottlieb LIPPISCH(*) (b.28 Sep 1751-Doelzschen,Germany;d.7 Jul 1817-Dresden,Germany)

      sp: A. M. NAUMANN(*) (b.Abt 1755-Germany;m.Abt 1776)

      4. Johann Gottlieb LIPPISCH(*) (b.15 Dec 1778-Kleinpestitz,Germany;d.26 Aug 1841-Kleinpestitz,Germany)

       sp: Johanna Christiana RUESTER(*) (b.16Sep1783-Gostritz,Germany;m.28 May1809;d.12Jun1865-Germany)

       5. Johanna F.Juliane Christiane LIPPISCH (b.6 Sep 1815-Kleinpestitz,Germany;d.23 Jul 1848-St. Louis,MO)

        sp: Johann Samuel Gottfried KAEMPFE (b.12 Oct 1811-Rippien, Germany;m.5 Feb 1837;d.9 Jun 1879-IL)

For Descendants of Juliane Christiane Lippisch and Johann Samuel Gottfried Kaempfe see Chapter Six

       5. Johann Gottlieb LIPPISCH(*) (b.6 May 1810-Kleinpestitz,Germany;d.28 Dec 1813-Leubnitz,Germany)

       5. Johanna Christiana LIPPISCH(*) (b.13 Aug 1811-Kleinpestitz,Germany;d.3 Sep 1811-Dresden,Germany)

       5. Johann Carl Traugott LIPPISCH(*) (b.27 Sep 1812-Kleinpestitz,Germany;d.20 Feb 1814-Leubnitz,Germany)

       5. Christiana Friederika LIPPISCH(*) (b.3 Mar 1817-Kleinpestitz,Dresden,Saxony,Germany)

       5. Amalia Christiana Friederika LIPPISCH(*) (b.1 Mar1819-Kleinpestitz,Germany;d.25 Aug1819-Dresden,Ger.)

       5. Johann Karl Gottlieb LIPPISCH(*) (b.16 Apr 1821-Kleinpestitz,Germany;d.22 May 1888-Dresden,Germany)

       5. Johanna Friederika Henriette LIPPISCH(*) (b.25 Jul1824-Kleinpestitz,Germany;d.29Jan1826-Dresden,Ger.)

     3. Johann George LIPPISCH(*) (b.4 Jul 1750-Doelzschen,Germany;d.6 Jul 1750-Dresden,Saxony,Germany)

     3. Female Child LIPPISCH(*) (b.6 Dec 1752-Doelzschen,Germany;d.6 Dec 1752-Dresden,Saxony,Germany

     3. Eva Regina LIPPISCH(*) (b.2 Feb 1754-Doelzschen,Germany;d.8 Oct 1761-Dresden,Saxony,Germany

     3. Johann George LIPPISCH(*) (b.12 May 1755-Doelzschen,Dresden,Saxony,Germany

     3. Christian Johann LIPPISCH(*) (b.1757;d.15 Nov 1813-Doelzschen,Dresden,Saxony,Germany)

     3. Anna Rosina LIPPISCH(*) (b.8 Sep 1758-Doelzschen,Germany;d.28 Nov 1797-Briesnitz,Saxony,Germany)

     3. Eva LIPPISCH(*) (b.4 Apr 1760-Doelzschen,Dresden,Saxony,Germany;d.4 Apr 1760-Dresden,Saxony,Germany)

   2. Maria LIPPISCH(*) (b.11 May 1724-Doelzschen,Dresden,Germany;d.9 Dec 1778-Rossthal,Saxony,Germany)

   2. Adam LIPPISCH(*) (b.15 Sep 1728-Doelzschen,Dresden,Saxony,Germany;d.11 Nov 1799

   2. Christian LIPPISCH(*) (b.29 Nov 1736-Doelzschen,Dresden,Germany;d.10 Oct 1798-Rossthal,Saxony,Germany)

> (*) Primary source is the Internet and is not verified.

CHAPTER SIX
DESCENDANTS OF SAMUEL GOTTFRIED KAEMPFE

1. Samuel Gottfried KAEMPFE(*) (b.Abt 1785-Germany)

  sp: Missis KAEMPFE(*) (b.Abt 1789-Germany;m.Abt 1810)

   2. Johanna Christiana KAEMPFE(**) (b.1 Jun 1806-Reppen,Dresden,Saxony,Germany;d.30 Apr 1879-Perry Co.,MO)

    sp: Johann Gottlieb PALISCH(**) (b.26 Oct 1805-Lobtau,Saxony,Germany;m.Abt 1827;d.3 Sep 1893-PerryCo.,MO)

   2. Johann Samuel Gottfried KAEMPFE (b.12 Oct 1811-Rippien,Dresden,Saxony,Germany;d.9 Jun 1879-Millstadt, IL)

    sp: Johanna F.Juliane Christiane LIPPISCH (b.6Sep 1815-Kleinpestitz,Ger.;m.5Feb1837;d.23Jul 1848-St. Louis,MO)

     3. Johann Samuel Gottfried KAEMPFE (Jr.) (b.4 Jun 1838-Kleinpestitz,Germany;d.15 Mar 1865-New Berne,NC)

     3. Traugott Gotthilf KAEMPFE (b.10 Aug 1840-Altenburg,Perry Co.,MO;d.11 Dec 1909-Frohna,Perry Co.,MO)

      sp: Justine Engel HENNECKE (b.2 May 1847-Centreville,St.Clair Co.,IL;m.7 May 1865;d.12Sep 1925-Frohna,MO)

       4. Louise Wilhelmine KAEMPFE (b.8 Feb 1866-Millstadt,St.Clair Co.,IL;d.28 Mar 1925-Frohna,Perry Co.,MO)

        sp: Claus STUEVE JR. (b.7 Mar 1863-Frohna,Perry Co.,MO;m.9 Apr1885;d.30 Jan1956-St. Louis,MO)

       4. Wilhelm Friedrich KAEMPFE (b.7 Nov 1868-Millstadt,St. Clair Co.,IL;d.7 Feb 1922-Farrar,Perry Co.,MO)

        sp: Anna Margaretha MANGELS (b.22 Sep 1872-Perry Co.,MO;m.29 Oct 1891;d.27 May 1939-Perry Co.,MO)

        5. Theobold Edmund KAEMPFE (b.18 Feb 1893-Frohna,Perry Co.,MO)

        5. Ella Olivia KAEMPFE (b.1 Aug 1895-Frohna,Perry Co.,MO)

        5. Paul KAEMPFE (b.Abt 1900-MO)

        5. Alfred KAEMPFE (b.Abt 1909-MO and thought to be still living in 2010)

       4. Otto Gottfried Traugott KAEMPFE (b.10 Dec 1870-Millstadt,St.ClairCo.,IL;d.3 Feb 1916-Frohna,Perry Co.,MO)

        sp: Martha Helene GEMEINHARDT (b.4Mar1880-Frohna,PerryCo.,MO;m.26Dec1912;d.1Mar1925-Frohna,MO)

        sp: Magdalena Dorothea MUELLER (b.17Jul1872-Frohna,PerryCo.,MO;m.3Oct 1895;d.3Aug1911-Frohna, MO)

        5. Joseph Traugott Martin KAEMPFE (b.21 Apr 1898-Frohna,Perry Co.,MO;d.8 Jan 1953-Perryville,MO)

         sp: Anna Maria MEYER (m.21 Apr 1919)

        5. Baby Girl KAEMPFE (b.9 Jul 1900-Frohna,Perry Co.,MO;d.9 Jul 1900)

        5. Walter Wilhelm Carl KAEMPFE (b.6 Mar 1902-Frohna,Perry Co.,MO;d.30 Oct 1969-Perryville,MO)

         sp: Bertha Clara Theodora BOEHME (b.12 Aug 1902-Farrar,MO;m.16 Apr1922;d.5 Aug 1966-Perryville,MO)

         6. Arlene Ruth (adopted) KAEMPFE

          sp: Robert Theodore BACHMANN (m.5 Apr 1953(Div))

           7. Cynthia Louise BACHMANN

            sp: Steven Hugo BRIGHAM (m.17 Jun 1974)

           7. Kirk Robert BACHMANN

            sp: Susan Jean WOLCZAK (m.19 Jun 1976)

           7. Lori Lynn BACHMANN

            sp: John L. HEINDENREICH (m.25 Nov 1989)

           7. Kathryn Ann BACHMANN

            sp: Richard Brian KLEPPIN (m.17 Jun 1983)

> (*) Primary source is the Internet and is not verified.
> (**) Relationship is not verified.

sp: Louise Ida GERHARDT

5. Theodor Johannes Ernst KAEMPFE (b.7 Sep 1905-Frohna,Perry Co.,MO;d.1987-Salina,KS)

   sp: Laura UNKNOWN

5. Albert Otto KAEMPFE (b.23 Mar 1909-Frohna,Perry Co.,MO)

   sp: Clara UNKNOWN

5. Rudolph Constantin KAEMPFE (b.20 Jun 1911-Frohna,Perry Co.,MO;d.2 Jul 1949-Frohna,Perry Co.,MO)

   sp: Lorene Salome HOEHN (m.18 May 1933)

4. Carl Johann KAEMPFE (b.9 May 1873-Millstadt,St. Clair Co.,IL;d.24 Jan 1946-Cape Girardeau,MO)

  sp: Frieda Emma Veronica BURFEIND (b.4 Feb 1879-Frohna,MO;m.27 Oct 1899;d.2 Aug 1949-CapeGir.,MO)

   5. Eugene Ottomar KAEMPFE (b.10 Mar 1901-Frohna,Perry Co.,MO;d.10 Apr 1929-Jefferson Co.,MO)

   5. Louise Hildegard KAEMPFE (b.18 Aug 1904-Frohna,Perry Co.,MO)

   5. Richard Ferdinand KAEMPFE (b.10 Jul 1907-Frohna,Perry Co.,MO;d.12 Dec 1992)

   5. Charles Traugott Herman KAEMPFE (b.1 Jun 1909-Frohna,Perry Co.,MO;d.23 Apr 1981)

   5. Amanda Frieda KAEMPFE (b.18 Apr 1911-Frohna,Perry Co.,MO)

   5. Mabel Myrtha KAEMPFE (b.26 Apr 1914-Frohna,Perry Co.,MO)

   5. Myrtle KAEMPFE (b.Abt 1917)

   5. Lillian E. KAEMPFE (b.Abt 1919)

   5. Dorthey R. KAEMPFE (b.Abt 1923)

4. Anna Justine Elisabethe KAEMPFE (b.12 Aug 1875-Millstadt,St. Clair Co.,IL;d.18 Dec 1954-Madison,NE)

  sp: Otto Friedrich OSWALD (b.26 Jun 1865-Chester,Logan Co.,IL;m.7 May 1893;d.1 Aug 1941-Frohna,MO)

   5. Alwin Waldemar OSWALD (b.23 Jun 1895-Frohna,Perry Co.,MO;d.8 Oct 1981-Lincoln,Lincoln Co.,KS)

    sp: Meta Adele Louise STROEMER (b.12 Dec 1895-Sylvan Grove,KS;m.20 Dec 1916;d.30 Aug 1979-KS)

    6. Ardis Bertha Anna OSWALD (b.31 Jul 1920-Sylvan Grove,Lincoln Co.,KS)

     sp: Roy JONES (b.Abt 1922)

      7. Lynda Eileen OSWALD

       sp: Thomas Francis RYAN (m.21 Jun 1970)

       8. David Lee RYAN

       8. Shannon Renee RYAN

       8. Nathan Shawn RYAN

     sp: Robert Lee FORTIN (b.22 Jan 1923-Augusta,MA;m.26 Dec 1966;d.18 Apr 1983-Sylvan Grove,KS)

     sp: Edwin William PEAVEY (b.30 Dec 1921-Beloit,KS;m.19 Mar 1963;d.17 Jan 1966-Wichita,KS)

    6. Florene Verna OSWALD (b.18 Mar 1923-Sylvan Grove,Lincoln Co.,KS)

     sp: Lawrence RINGLER (b.15 Apr 1914-Bunker Hill,KS;m.29 Jun 1947;d.30 Aug 1998-Emporia,KS)

      7. Patrick James RINGLER

      7. Darrell Dean RINGLER

       sp: Lea Ann MARKOWITZ (m.20 Aug 1977)

       8. Amy Beth RINGLER

8. Lauren Jean RINGLER

7. Carol Jean RINGLER

  sp: Ted Stuart PASSMORE m.14 May 1972)

  8. Bruce Ted PASSMORE

  8. Matthew Stuart PASSMORE

7. John Phillip RINGLER

  sp: Valerie Gale PHIPPS (m.4 Aug 1974)

  8. Tyler John RINGLER

  8. Chelsea Gale RINGLER

5. Anna OSWALD (b.6 Dec 1897-Frohna,Perry Co.,MO;d.6 Dec 1897-Frohna,Perry Co.,MO)

5. Alfred Reinhold OSWALD (b.23 Jan 1900-Frohna,Perry Co.,MO;d.1995-Madison,NE)

  sp: Minnie OETTING (b.19 Feb 1898;d.Mar 2000)

  6. Lloyd OSWALD

    sp: UNKNOWN

    7. Terry OSWALD

    7. David OSWALD

5. Ervin Martin OSWALD (b.16 Jul 1907-Frohna,Perry Co.,MO;d.20 Dec 1985-Wayne,NE)

  sp: Roberta L. POPP (b.9 Sep 1912-Frohna,Perry Co.,MO;m.7 May 1933)

  6. Edward OSWALD

    sp: UNKNOWN

    7. Douglas OSWALD

    7. Daniel OSWALD

    7. Dennis OSWALD

  6. Lois OSWALD

    sp: Donald ETZEL

    7. Curtis ETZEL

  6. Vernon OSWALD

    sp: Rita Renee KNOP (m.27 Jun 1971)

    7. Scott Vernon OSWALD

    7. Amy Renee OSWALD

    7. Jill Marie OSWALD

5. Paul Gotthilf OSWALD (b.22 Mar 1910-Frohna,Perry Co.,MO;d.11 Jan 1993-Madison,NE)

  sp: Viola MILLER (m.23 Jun 1946)

  6. Harold OSWALD

  6. Ardell OSWALD

  6. Merlin OSWALD

  6. Brian OSWALD

      6. Allen OSWALD

      6. Marie OSWALD

4. Heinrich Ernst KAEMPFE (b.13 May 1878-Frohna,Perry Co.,MO;d.10 Nov 1952-Frohna,Perry Co.,MO)

4. Theodor Samuel KAEMPFE (b.28 Jun 1882-Frohna,Perry Co.,MO;d.13 Dec 1963-Cape Girardeau,MO)

  sp: Lina Christina KOENIG (b.15 Jan 1887-New Wells,MO;m.8 Nov 1906;d.26 Dec 1955-Shrewsbury,MO)

    5. Reinhold Albert KAEMPFE (b.6 Nov 1907-Frohna,Perry Co.,MO;d.5 Dec 1987-Frohna,Perry Co. MO)

      sp: Louisa SCHADE (b.26 Apr 1906;d.3 Feb 1999-St. Louis,MO)

      6. Wilma L. SCHADE (b.Abt Dec 1925-MO)

      6. LaVern SCHADE

      6. Delores M. SCHADE

        sp: Carl E. FADLER

    5. Paula Anita KAEMPFE (b.21 Jan 1910-Frohna,Perry Co.,MO;d.31 Jul 1995-Frohna,Perry Co. MO)

      sp: Alvin MEYER (b.2 Jun 1904;m.14 Apr 1940;d.May 1981)

      6. Imogene R. MEYER

        sp: Thomas "Jerry" J. UNGER

        7. Gregory UNGER

        7. Thomas UNGER

      6. Courtney MEYER

        sp: Connie KIRCHNER

        7. Caleb MEYER

        7. Joshua MEYER

        7. Anna MEYER

      6. Marvis C. MEYER

        sp: Sally A. LETTEER

      6. Pearline MEYER

        sp: Larry DEGENHARDT

        7. Grant DEGENHARDT

        7. Ryan DEGENHARDT

        7. Tyler DEGENHARDT

        7. Clay DEGENHARDT

      6. Ritha C. MEYER

        sp: Bruce G. HACKER

      sp: Ernst W. VERSEMAN (b.14 Apr 1900-Perry Co.,MO;d.18 May 1998-Frohna,Perry Co. MO)

    5. Alida Justine KAEMPFE (b.2 May 1913-Frohna,Perry Co.,MO;d.26 Dec 1995-Chesterfield,MO)

    5. Raymond Hugo KAEMPFE (b.13 Sep 1917-Frohna,Perry Co.,MO;d.7 Jul 1971-Altenburg,MO)

      sp: Olga Sophia HAERTLING (b.27 Dec 1912-New Wells,MO;m.16 Jan 1944;d.30 Mar 1978-Altenburg,MO)

      6. Betty Jean KAEMPFE

6. Faye Marie KAEMPFE (b.5 Feb 1949-New Wells,MO;d.7 Feb 1949-Cape Girardeau,MO)

5. Otto Harold KAEMPFE (b.14 Apr 1920-Frohna,Perry Co.,MO;d.29 May 1940-Frohna,Perry Co.,MO)

5. Elton Theobold KAEMPFE (b.15 Jul 1922-Frohna,Perry Co.,MO;d.26 Aug 1925-Frohna,Perry Co.,MO)

5. Milda Doris KAEMPFE (b.18 Mar 1925-Frohna,Perry Co.,MO;d.13 Apr 2008-St. Louis Co.,MO)

  sp: Charles Joseph MONTI Sr. (b.28 Nov 1920-St.Louis,MO;m.6 Jul 1946;d.27 Jun 2006-St. Louis Co.,MO)

  6. Charles Joseph MONTI Jr.

    sp: Vasana N. MALITONG-SIMON-CUNNINGHAM (m.17 Jul 1981)

    7. May Lynn (Cunningham) MONTI (adopted)

  6. Carmelo Louis MONTI AIA

    sp: Mary Linda MILLER (m.1 Sep 1979)

    7. Jason Miller MONTI

  6. Michael James MONTI

    sp: Mary POLITTE-MCGOWAN (m.17 Aug 1974(Div))

    7. Candace Lee MONTI

    7. Michelle (McGowan) MONTI (Adopted)

    7. Paul Michael (McGowan) MONTI (Adopted)

  6. Paul Stephen MONTI

    sp: Ellen Marie VEIT (m.7 Aug 1976(Div))

    7. Victoria Lynn MONTI

    7. Stephen Paul MONTI

    sp: Marsha Lynn SUMNER-REAGAN (m.23 Jun 1990)

    7. Rebecca Lynn REAGAN

    7. Isaac David REAGAN

    7. Sarah Beth REAGAN

    7. Jacob Warren REAGAN

  6. Sheila Christine MONTI

    sp: Jose MOLINA (m.27 Dec 1985)

    7. Molly MOLINA (stepdaughter)

  6. Mark Edward MONTI

    sp: Kathleen A. SCANLON (b.7 Oct 1960;m.11 Feb 1984(Div);d.4 Feb 2008-Affton,St. Louis Co.,MO)

    7. Christopher Joseph MONTI

    7. Kayla Christine MONTI

    sp: Audra THOMAS (m.24 Apr 2007)

5. Regina Gladys KAEMPFE (b.7 Mar 1928-Frohna,Perry Co.,MO;d.12 Mar 1928-Frohna,Perry Co.,MO)

4. Charlotte Catharine Mathilde KAEMPFE (b.4 Oct 1884-Frohna,Perry Co.,MO)

  sp: Joseph Hermann STUEVE (b.22 May 1882-Frohna,Perry Co.,MO;m.6 Nov 1904;d.Oct 1967-Enid,OK)

  5. Leona STUEVE (b.Abt 1906-Kansas)

5. Alma STUEVE (b.23 Sep 1909-Kansas;d.29 Apr 2002-Tulsa,Tulsa Co.,OK)

5. Theodore STUEVE (b.17 Oct 1911-Kansas;d.30 Aug 1995-Pueblo,CO)

3. Ernst Leberecht KAEMPFE (b.15 Jul 1842-Altenburg,Perry Co.,MO;d.19 Aug 1842-Altenburg,Perry Co.,MO)

3. Carl August KAEMPFE (b.15 Jul 1842-Altenburg,Perry Co.,MO;d.26 Apr 1844-St. Louis,MO)

3. Christian Ferdinand KAEMPFE (b.13 Jan 1845-Millstadt,St. Clair Co.,IL;d.16 Nov 1848-St. Louis,MO)

3. Gottlieb Daniel KAEMPFE (b.19 Mar 1847-St. Louis,MO;d.14 Apr 1847-St. Louis,MO)

3. Pauline Elisabeth KAEMPFE (b.2 Apr 1848-St. Louis,MO;d.12 Aug 1848-St. Louis,MO)

sp: Christiane MUELLER (b.24 Mar 1819-Brombach,Nassau,Saxony,Germany;m.1 Jan 1850;d.3 Feb 1875-IL)

3. Wilhelm Ludwig KAEMPFE (b.18 Mar 1851-Millstadt,St. Clair Co.,IL;d.31 Jan 1878-Millstadt,St. Clair Co.,IL)

sp: Juliane HOFSTETTER (b.21 Jun 1851-St. Clair Co.,IL;m.1 Jan 1871;d.18 Mar 1880-IL)

3. Johann Gottfried KAEMPFE (b.28 Mar 1853-Millstadt,St. Clair Co.,IL;d.6 Feb 1938)

sp: Charlotte Wilhelmine HASKENHOFF (b.18 Mar 1856-Hannover,Germany;m.17 May 1874;d.31 Oct 1892)

4. William John KAEMPFE (b.19 Apr 1875-Millstadt,St. Clair Co.,IL;d.31 Oct 1934-Lafayette Co.,MO)

4. Gottfried KAEMPFE (b.8 Oct 1876;d.8 Jun 1877)

4. Marie Caroline KAEMPFE (b.27 Aug 1878-Centreville,St.Clair Co.,IL;d.28 Feb 1952-Belleville,St..Clair Co.,IL)

sp: Martin Joseph HOOCK (b.25 Aug 1873-St. Clair Co.,IL;m.7 Jan 1900;d.8 Jan 1957-East St. Louis, IL)

5. Bernice Emily HOOCK (b.29 Jul 1909-Cahokia,St. Clair Co.,IL;d.12 Jul 1990-Cahokia,St. Clair Co.,IL)

4. Louis J. KAEMPFE (b.27 Feb 1879;d.8 Jul 1879)

4. Carl Adam "Charles" KAEMPFE (b.25 Sep 1880-Sugar Loaf Twp.,St. Clair Co.,IL;d.7 Nov 1971)

sp: Caroline N. HOFSTETTER (b.30 Nov 1884-Sugar Loaf Twp.,St.Clair Co.,IL;m.14 Oct 1903;d.10 Jan 1971)

4. Emilie Magdalena "Amelia" KAEMPFE (b.22 Mar 1886-Centreville Twp.,St. Clair Co.,IL;d.5 Dec 1964)

sp: William Peter HOFSTETTER (b.22 Mar 1882-St. Clair Co.,IL;m.1 Jun 1905;d.26 Jun 1963-St. Clair Co.,IL)

5. Leroy Karl HOFSTETTER (b.18 Apr 1906-Illinois;d.20 Jul 1986-Columbia,Monroe Co.,IL)

5. Erma Louise HOFSTETTER (b.23 Apr 1910-Columbia,Monroe Co.,IL;d.9 Mar 1993-Columbia,IL)

sp: Louisa MEYER(*) (b.1866;m.26 Oct 1893;d.1923)

3. Marie Magdalene KAEMPFE (b.12 Jan 1855-Millstadt,St. Clair Co.,IL;d.28 Nov 1932)

sp: Jacob Adam HOFSTETTER (b.20 Jun 1848-St. Clair Co.,IL;m.16 Jan 1872;d.27 May 1914-Millstadt,IL)

4. Christiane Caroline HOFSTETTER (b.26 Dec 1872-St. Clair Co.,IL;d.29 Apr 1873-St. Clair Co.,IL)

4. Friedrich Adam HOFSTETTER (b.18 Jan 1876-St. Clair Co.,IL;d.22 Apr 1876-St. Clair Co.,IL)

4. Louise Wilhelmine Magdalena HOFSTETTER (b.6 Jan 1877-Sugar Loaf Twp.,St. Clair Co.,IL;d.8 Sep 1878)

4. Wilhelmina "Minnie" Christine HOFSTETTER (b.17 Oct 1878-Sugar Loaf Twp.,St. Clair Co.,IL;d.28 Mar 1943)

sp: Ralph STOUT (b.Oct 1874-St. Clair Co.,IL;m.19 Jan 1898;d.1965)

4. Jacob HOFSTETTER (b.29 Dec 1879-Sugar Loaf Twp.,St. Clair Co.,IL;d.Jun 1880-Columbia,Monroe Co.,IL)

4. Jacob Freidrich HOFSTETTER (b.10 Aug 1881-St. Clair Co.,IL;d.25 Dec 1945-Belleville, St. Clair Co.,IL)

sp: Mary HARRIS (b.Aug 1881-Sugar Loaf Twp.,St. Clair Co.,IL;m.12 Jul 1904;d.10 Mar 1959-St. Louis,MO)

4. Maria Magdalena HOFSTETTER (b.10 Aug 1883-St. Clair Co.,IL;d.12 Sep 1883-St. Clair Co.,IL)

4. George HOFSTETTER (b.10 Aug 1883-St. Clair Co.,IL;d.6 Jun 1971-Belleville,St. Clair Co.,IL)

sp: Emma STRAUSS (b.2 Mar 1888-Millstadt,St. Clair Co.,IL;m.9 Dec 1911;d.3 Sep 1978-Millstadt,IL)

4. Marie Margarete HOFSTETTER (b.30 May 1885-St. Clair Co.,IL;d.1 Oct 1974-Waterloo,Monroe Co.,IL)

  sp: Melvin Lee STEPHENS (b.3 Jun 1886-Sugar Loaf Twp.,St. Clair Co.,IL;m.Aft 1932;d.Oct 1976-Waterloo,IL)

  sp: William Frank STRAUB (b.29 Mar 1879-St. Louis,MO;m.24 Dec 1904(Div);d.13 Dec 1958)

4. Adam HOFSTETTER (b.3 Nov 1887-Sugar Loaf Twp.,St. Clair Co.,IL;d.9 Nov 1889-St. Clair Co.,IL)

4. Hermann HOFSTETTER (b.30 Jun 1889-St. Clair Co.,IL;d.8 Feb 1937-Cement Hollow,St. Clair Co.,IL)

  sp: Frieda LEPERE (b.7 Oct 1889-Sugar Loaf Twp.,St. Clair Co.,IL;m.7 Aug 1915;d.27 Dec 1950)

4. Friedrich Wilhelm HOFSTETTER (b.20 Feb 1891-St. Clair Co.,IL;d.13 Jun 1906-Millstadt, St. Clair Co., IL)

4. Capitola Pauline HOFSTETTER (b.8 Dec 1894-St. Clair Co.,IL;d.25 Aug 1942-Waterloo,Monroe Co.,IL)

  sp: John W. BUETTNER (b.6 Apr 1883-Waterloo,Monroe Co.,IL;m.Abt 1915;d.7 Aug 1936-Wartburg,IL)

4. Edwin Georg Oscar HOFSTETTER (b.16Jan1898-Sugar Loaf Twp.,St.ClairCo.,IL;d.28Feb1980-St. Louis,MO)

3. Christine Elisabethe KAEMPFE (b.20 Feb 1857-Millstadt,St. Clair Co.,IL;d.12 Nov 1873-Millstadt,St. Clair Co.,IL)

3. Still Born KAEMPFE (b.25 Sep 1860-Millstadt,St. Clair Co.,IL;d.25 Sep 1860-Millstadt,St. Clair Co.,IL)

Note: Christiane MUELLER (see page 36) was previously married to Unknown MOOS and widowed before marrying the widower Johann Samuel Gottfried KAEMPFE on Jan. 1, 1850. She had three children with Moos:

  Joh. Friedr. Theodor "Fred" MOOS (b. 27 Jan. 1842, Nassau Germany; d. 20 May 1869)

  Dorothea Henrett. Wil. "Mimma" MOOS (b. 3 Jul 1843, Nassau, Germany)

  Joh. Phillip MOOS (b. 6 Oct 1848; Millstatdt, IL; d. 2 Feb 1856, Millstadt, IL)

She and Samuel then had five children in Millstadt, Illinois between 1851 and 1860, but only three survived to adulthood and married.

Edward Wilhelm and Juliana Mathilda (Reuschel) Koenig
Circa 1916
Photos courtesy of Milda (Kaempfe) Monti Estate

PART TWO

KOENIG - REUSCHEL

Heraldic Symbols for Two Ancestral Towns

Korbussen

This heraldic symbol is associated with Korbussen, Uranlagerstatte Ronnenberg, Gera, Thuringen, Deutschland (Germany) from which several Koenigs emigrated. The area is 25% forested, with timber being an important product, and is known for its minerals, including dolomite and uranium.

Ronneburg

This heraldic symbol contains a weaving shuttle because, at one time, textiles were an important part of the area's economy. The lion derives from part of the coat of arms of the Reuss family. The area was heavily mined for uranium by the Soviets from 1953 to 1990.

Ancestors of Lina Christina KOENIG

⌐ Andreas KOENIG

⌐ Christian KOENIG (b.27 Sep 1799-Korbusssen,Thuringen,Germany;m.13 Feb 1823;d.20 Aug 1877-Korbusssen,Germany)

Andreas KOENIG (b.12 Jul 1825-Korbussen,Saxe-Altenburg,Thuringia,Germany;m.21 Mar 1854;d.13 Jan 1886-New Wells,MO)

⌐ Johann KIRMSE

Maria KIRMSE (b.8 Mar 1802-Muerken,Thuringen,Germany;d.18 May 1865-Korbusssen,Thuringen,Germany)

Edward Wilhelm KOENIG (b.10 Jan 1861-Frohna,Perry Co.,MO;m.24 Apr 1884;d. 7 Sep 1944-Altenburg,Perry Co.,MO)

⌐ Johann HAERTLING (b.19 Sep 1776-Korbusssen,Thuringen,Germany;m.8 Jul 1800;d.3 Feb 1841-Poeppeln,Thuringen,Ger.)

Andreas HAERTLING (b.27 Mar 1805-Poeppeln,Thuringen,Germany;m.26 Apr 1831;d.30 Mar 1877-Poeppeln,Thuringen,Ger.)

Regina NUENDEL (b.24 Aug 1779-Poeppeln,Thuringen,Germany;d.18 Apr 1845-Poeppeln,Thuringen,Germany)

Christina Justina HAERTLING (b.17 Sep 1831-Poeppeln,Saxe-Altenburg,T,Germany;d.26 Jul 1890-New Wells,CapeGirar.Co.,MO)

⌐ Christian ALBRECHT

Maria ALBRECHT (b.Abt 1809-Baldenhain,Thuringen,Germany;d.15 May 1844-Poeppeln,Thuringen,Germany)

Lina Christina KOENIG (b.15 Jan 1887-New Wells,Cape Girardeau Co.,MO;d.26 Dec 1955-Shrewsbury,St.LouisCo.,MO)

⌐ Georg REUSCHEL (d.Bef 1857)

⌐ Friederick Bernhardt REUSCHEL (b.Abt 1831-Scheosswieths,Seesen,Altenburg,Germany;m.15 Sep 1857;d.Bef Nov 1864)

Juliana Mathilda REUSCHEL (b.1 Mar 1862-Wittenburg,Perry Co.,MO;d.26 Mar 1921-Brazeau Township,Perry Co.,MO)

⌐ Gottlieb SIERMANN (d.Bef 1857)

Friederika Emilia SIERMANN (b.Abt 1837-Missouri or Germany;d.Abt 1865)

Lina Christiana Koenig
November 8, 1906
Lina and her husband Theodor Samuel Kaempfe bought the farm near Frohna, MO after the death of Theodor's father Traugott, around 1910.

Photo courtesy of Miller-Monti Collection

CHAPTER SEVEN

ANCIENT HISTORY AND EMIGRATION
OF
FOUR GERMAN ANCESTORS

Haertling, Koenig, Reuschel, and Siermann

As noted in the Introduction, four ancestors of Lina Christina Koenig came from three small agricultural villages in the Duchy of Saxe-Altenburg, which is part of (3) **Thuringia**, Germany. Their dates of birth and death are incomplete but cities of origin are known. For some, there are enough details to construct a small picture of their lives, but none as complete as for the Kaempfes.

Andreas Koenig was born in Korbussen (called "Corbrissen by Ronneburg" in church records); his wife Christina Haertling came from neighboring Poeppeln; and Gottlieb Siermann came from Heukewalde. Frederick Bernhardt Reuschel also probably came from this area, but his available information is unclear.

The Thuringians were a tribe occupying land between the Elbe and the Danube Rivers. They were conquered by the Franks in the sixth century and converted to Christianity in the eighth century. Charlemagne placed Thuringia as a frontier state between him and the Slavs, but by the tenth century Saxon dukes had wrested control. During the Holy Roman Empire, rulers changed frequently culminating with the division of Thuringia into duchies in 1485. In 1815 the duchies became members of the German Confederation. Eventually they again merged into the state of Thuringia, and today it is the most densely populated state in modern Germany.

Thus arose the Thuringian Duchy of Saxe-Altenburg, an area of about two hundred square miles, bordering Saxony. The larger towns of Gera and Ronneburg (with its impressive castle) are near its eastern border, and the small towns of Heukewalde, Korbussen, and Poeppeln are not far away. As such, they have been at various times part of Saxony, depending on the whim of nobles. This area is particularly fertile so agriculture was its primary industry for centuries. Heukewalde, about eight miles east of Ronneburg, was first documented as a town in 1152. Houses are still built with a typical Altenburger framework of exposed heavy oak half-timbers with white plaster in between. Several have been converted in recent years into hotels for the tourist industry. The town is quaint with a quiet idyllic rural setting.

Gottlieb Siermann emigrated from this environment to the U. S., but when and why are unknown. Trinity Lutheran Church records for Altenburg, Perry County, Missouri, show that in 1857, his "only daughter" Frederika Emilia Siermann married Frederick Bernhardt Reuschel. Her father is noted as "the late Gottlieb Siermann from Heukewalde." Gottlieb is never mentioned again, but the Trinity records do contain another Siermann who could have been his sister. She was Hana Sophia (Siermann) Krause, and in 1855 she gave birth to her seventh child in Altenburg, Missouri. A good guess would be that Gottlieb had come to America in the early 1850's with his family, and perhaps his sister's family. His only daughter Frederika Emilia probably emigrated with him as a child. Her date of birth is unknown.

Not far away, about three miles north of Ronneburg, lay the twin villages of Poeppeln and Korbussen. Little is known of their origin, but their history probably followed that of Ronneburg, and it was a difficult one. Foundations of a fortress date to 800 A.D., but most of the buildings and walls have long been dismantled or ruined. Politically, the area has changed hands many times, going from Saxon to Thuringian as recently as 1920. In 1665 and in 1829, major fires nearly leveled Ronneburg. In 1611, the plague killed hundreds. In 1632 the villages were plundered by Imperial troops during the Thirty Years War. In 1766, sulphur springs were discovered, and mineral baths were built, providing a new source of income for the impoverished area. In 1953, the Soviet Union began mining uranium ore, and this had devastating effects on the surrounding area. Huge mounds of spent ore disrupted the once beautiful countryside. Nearby towns of Reust and Paitzdorf received particularly large mounds. Korbussen was the

Andreas Koenig 1825-1886
Notice similarities with drawing on page 46
Image courtesy of Morgan (Meyr) Lake

location of one of the pit mines, so Poeppeln was likely affected as well. Since 1990, the mining has stopped and steps are being taken to clean up the environmental damage.

Nelson A. Haertling is a descendant of Christine's brother Hermann, and he has been to Poeppeln and Korbussen. He reported that all direct line descendants of the ancestral Haertlings were killed in World War Two, but, miraculously, the house where the Haertlings lived is still standing and is occupied by some relatives named Koenig and Hahn. He copied many of the Korbussen church records and provided copies of some for this report. As a result, two earlier generations are documented in the ancestry charts.

Koenig, Haertling, Reuschel, and Siermann are not mentioned in Forster's book *Zion on the Mississippi*, which describes in detail the emigration history of the Stephanites from Germany to Missouri. However, their German places of birth and other nearby related towns (Poeppeln, Heukewalde, Gera, Ronneburg, Reust and Paitzdorf) are mentioned in connection with a small group of one hundred forty-one followers from Saxe-Altenburg who stayed behind in Germany for a year, traveled separately, arrived in Perry County in December 1839, and settled in Paitzdorf (later Uniontown), Missouri. They formed Grace Lutheran Church in February 1840.

Church records for Grace show the marriage of Andreas Koenig and Christine (*sic*) Haertling, March 21, 1854, and that they were married in private due to the season of Lent. He was thirty years old and she was twenty-two. Comments show that Andreas came to the USA in 1853; that he was single and living at Kimmels Mills in St. Genevieve County; that he was "born at Corbrissen, near Ronneburg County, Altenburg, Saxon, Germany"; that sponsors Christian Magwitz and Friedrich Koenig signed his release papers to come to America; that he was the second son and the second child. The comments then show that Christine was "born at Pappeln near Ronneburg County, Altenburg, Saxon, Germany" and that she was the first daughter and first child of Andreas Haertling. Furthermore, Nelson Haertling said that the church records in Korbussen show that she was baptized there because there was no church in Poeppeln; and that she and her next younger sister Maria came unmarried to Missouri, but no ship's registry has been found to set the date. Later in 1866, their younger brother Hermann Haertling immigrated and soon married Sophie Koenig, a niece to Andreas Koenig. Obviously, the Koenig and Haertling families were closely connected due to the proximity of their native villages and the history of the other Stephanites from Saxe-Altenburg.

One last note to this area is in reference to Frederick Bernhardt Reuschel. As noted above, the Trinity church records list the marriage between "Friedr. Bernhard Reuschel, oldest son of the late Georg Reuschel from Scheosswieths, in Seesen (*sic*) by Altenburg" to Emilia Siermannin 1857 in Perry County, Missouri. Georg Reuschel is never mentioned again. Further, an e-mail from Morgan (Meyr) Lake, a descendant of Andreas Koenig and his son Alvin Koenig, states, "At the archive center (in Jackson, Missouri), they have a naturalization document for Bernhardt Reuschel dated 5 Feb. 1855 from Sax-Altenburg, age twenty-three." That would place his birth year at 1831 or 1832, depending on month, and clearly in Thuringia.

The names given for his place of origin are in conflict with one another and with the naturalization record. Seesen is a town in the province of Hanover in the Kingdom of Prussia, and it is nowhere near the city of Altenburg, Saxe-Altenburg. Therefore, it seems likely that the name "Seesen by Altenburg" is a corruption of "Sachsen-Altenburg" which is German for Saxe-Altenburg. Furthermore, the name Scheosswieths never shows up in any search conducted on the Internet so it could be grossly misspelled, or it could have ceased to exist long ago. Also, his last name "Reuschel" seems connected to the many towns in the Ronneburg area that begin with "Reus" and the nearby, very small, historical Duchy of Reuss. Dating to the twelfth century, "Reeves" were hired to protect the heavily forested kingdom; the word eventually became a

Marriage License
Edward Koenig and Julia Reuschel (*sic*)

License was dated April 15, 1884 and marriage took place on April 24, 1884 at Evangelical Lutheran Church in New Wells, Cape Girardeau County, Missouri

Image courtesy of Morgan (Meyr) Lake

family name and further divided to include the Reuss family name, which was the only line to survive to the twentieth century. In 1919 the region was called Reuss but was later absorbed into Thuringia. Therefore, Georg Reuschel probably came from the same area of Saxe-Altenburg as Koenig, Haertling, and Siermann, for similar reasons to those of the Stephanites: religious freedom and economic opportunity.

Unknown Woman

One intriguing mystery involves the drawing of an Unknown Woman that was owned by Milda (Kaempfe) Monti. The drawing was heavily damaged and in the late 1900s her son Carmelo Monti had the image scanned and touched up digitally to remove a major tear. That image appears on page 46 and Milda identified her as Juliana Mathilda (Reuschel) Koenig. However, the drawing itself bears many similarities to the drawing of Andreas Koenig provided by Morgan (Meyr) Lake on page 42. Could the Unknown Woman actually be Christina Justina (Haertling) Koenig, wife of Andreas Koenig?

CHAPTER EIGHT

POST-IMMIGRATION HISTORY FOR TWO GERMAN COUPLES

Koenig / Haertling and Reuschel / Siermann

The post-immigration history of these two ancestral couples is nearly as complete as that of Kaempfe/Lippisch, but it's not as detailed. Census records were viewed; church records exist for some of them; but no books have been written which specifically include them. Many of these details along with oral history came together to create an interesting, albeit, limited picture.

Koenig / Haertling

In their emigration history, speculatively, this couple's families were probably connected due to the very close proximity of their native villages, Korbussen and Poeppeln, in Saxe-Altenburg, Thuringia. Andreas Koenig had come as a single person in 1853 to Kimmels Mills, Missouri, with the permission of two "sponsors" in Germany. He married Christina Justina Haertling (age twenty-two) on March 21, 1854, at Grace Lutheran Church in Paitzdorf (Uniontown), Missouri when he was thirty. While living in that area, Andreas and Christine had three children, but only one, Julius Koenig, born Oct. 15, 1857, would survive beyond infancy.

Later, the 1860 U. S. census for Missouri, Perry County, Brazeau Township, Perryville Post Office, shows Andreas Koenig (age 36) as a farmer with $1000 in real estate and $400 in personal property, born in "Sax. Altenburg." Other family members include Justina (27) also born in "Sax. Altenburg," Julius (2) born in Missouri, and Anna Sander (11) born in "Sax-Altenburg." Church records for Concordia Lutheran Church in Frohna, Missouri, show the baptism of three Koenig children: Eduard (*sic*) Wilhelm (b. 1-10-1861), Maria Martha (b. 11-1-1862), and Benjamine (b. 11-29-1864). There is also one death record, that of three-years-and-nine-months-old Eduard Koenig, born at Paitzdorf, who died on January 10, 1860. There is a good chance Eduard (*sic*) Wilhelm born later in 1861 was named after the deceased Eduard because his birthday coincided with his younger brother's date of death.

Sometime between the birth of Benjamine in 1864 and the 1868 Missouri State Census for Cape Girardeau County, the Koenig family moved from Frohna to New Wells. Two photographs of their homestead at New Wells show a nice-sized two-story house with an overhanging front porch. Alvin Koenig was born there on March 30, 1868, and lived there his entire life. In the 1868 census, Andrew Koenig (age 21-45) is a head of household. Other members are Christena (21-45), Julius (6-10), Edward (6-10), Mary (6-10), Benjamin (-10), and Alwin (-10). Notice the Americanization of the names by the census taker. Then in 1874, Eduard (*sic*) Koenig was confirmed at Immanuel Evangelical Lutheran Church in New Wells.

Above: **Unknown Woman**
May be Juliana Mathilda (Reuschel) Koenig
(See page 44) Image courtesy of Carmelo L. Monti
Left: **Koenig Homestead**
New Wells, Cape Girardeau County
Photos courtesy of Morgan (Meyr) Lake

The 1876 Missouri State Census for Cape Girardeau County lists a family headed by Andreas Koenig (age 45+). Other family members are Christine (45+), Julius (21-45), Edward (10-18), Benjamine (10-18), and Alvin (-10). Susan Felwar (-10) is next on the list and is probably the same Susana Felway who appears later in the 1880 census. Living next door is a family of Hartlings (*sic*) – probably the Americanized spelling of Haertling.

Notice that Maria Martha (or Mary) is missing, without explanation. An Individual File online at familysearch.org shows Maria Martha Koenig's death date as Aug. 30, 1874. If this were the same person as the child born to Andreas on November 1, 1861, then obviously she would not appear in census records after 1874. However, the online Missouri Birth and Death Records Database shows Marie Martha (Koenig) Koenig being married to Herman Koenig and giving birth in 1885 in Saline Township of Perry County. Note that in 1868 there was a young Herman Koenig living next to the Andrew Koenig household. Therefore, it is possible, but unverified, that this Marie Martha is the sister of Edward Koenig. Milda (Kaempfe) Monti granddaughter of Edward, stated that she had several Koenig cousins in the area around Frohna but could no longer recall how they were connected.

The 1880 United States Census online at familysearch.org shows the Andrew Koenig household with nine people (Andrew, Augustena, Julius, Edward, Benjamine, Alwin, and Elizabeth Koenig and Susana Felway and Henry Keiser). Andrew's occupation is shown as farmer. The census place is shown as Shawnee, Cape Girardeau County, Missouri. Shawnee is a geographical subdivision of the county where the town of New Wells is located.

Andrew's great-granddaughter Milda (Kaempfe) Monti confirmed that her grandfather Edward Koenig had three brothers, Jules, Ben and Alvin, and that there was a laborer named Henry who had lived with them a long time. As a youngster, she wrote letters to Henry for Edward, because Henry had moved to Hermann, Missouri. She remembered traveling to the Koenig homestead by buggy from Frohna, and crossing Apple Creek, a frightening experience for a child. She did not recognize any of the women's names on the 1880 census. One woman, Augustena, is probably Andrew's wife Christina Justina. A second woman, Elizabeth, is shown as a daughter-in-law and is probably Julie Elizabeth Loos, the wife of the oldest son Julius. The third, Susana Felway age ten, is completely unknown. She is shown as a daughter so it is possible that she was an orphan and the Koenigs took her in to rear.

On April 24, 1884, the Cape Girardeau Co. Recorder of Deeds and church records for Immanuel Evangelical Lutheran Church in New Wells, Missouri, list the marriage between Edward Koenig and Julia Reuschel. See reproduction on page 44.

Morgan (Meyr) Lake, a descendent of Andreas Koenig and his son Alvin, provided information about Andreas and Christine Justina (Haertling) Koenig, including their dates and places of birth, death, and marriage, and photographs of Andreas and his homestead. Andreas died on January 13, 1886 and was buried in New Wells. Morgan indicated that the "Will" for Andreas Koenig is in the Cape Girardeau County Archives in Jackson, Missouri, in the Cape County Circuit Clerk Wills Book D, page 478, #2069, and Julius Koenig and Herman Haertling were the witnesses. In it, Andreas left parcels of land in New Wells to Wilhelm Eduard (*sic*) Koenig. Christine continued living in the family homestead until her death on July 26, 1890. On a 1900's property owner's map, all the brothers had farms near each other. Alvin, who had suffered for a long time from squamous cell carcinoma of the throat that rendered him speechless, lived in the homestead with his family until his death in 1940 at age seventy-one.

The 1920 census lists Edward Koenig at age fifty-nine with Julia (*sic*) as his wife and a daughter Natellie (*sic*) in Shawnee Township, Cape Girardeau County, Missouri. Edward's birthplace is shown as Missouri, but his parents were both from Germany.

On March 26, 1921 Juliana (Reuschel) Koenig died at age fifty-nine from apoplexy due to cerebral hemorrhage (a stroke) in Frohna, but she was buried in the New Wells Cemetery. Her son-in-law Theodore (*sic*) Kaempfe gave the information for her death certificate and his spelling of her parents' names (Bernhardt Reusherg and Emilie Nascher both from Germany) deviates considerably from the 1857 Trinity church records described on page 48. The 1930 census online at Ancestry.com lists Edward Koenig at age sixty-nine with a housekeeper named

Alvine Best in Shawnee Township, Cape Girardeau County, Missouri. In 1940, Edward was listed as a surviving brother in Alvin's obituary. On September 7, 1944 Edward Wilhelm Koenig died at age eighty-three in Altenburg, Missouri, after suffering for six weeks from gangrene of his lower left leg, and he's buried in Trinity Lutheran Church Cemetery in Altenburg.

Reuschel / Siermann

In their immigration history, this couple was first seen marrying at Trinity Lutheran Church in Altenburg on September 15, 1857. Frederick Bernhardt Reuschel was about twenty-five, but Frederika Emilia Siermann's age is unknown. Those same church records go on to list Juliana Mathilde Reuschel as their first child, born on March 1, 1862.

Trinity Lutheran Church
Altenbury, Perry County, Missouri
Photo by Mary L. Miller

Then on page 149, the Trinity Church records list the marriage between "Emilie Reuschel, a widow, and Gottlieb Schuessler on November 10, 1864." There is no listing for the death of Bernhardt Reuschel, but page 183 notes that no death records were found for April 13, 1864 to November 6, 1876. Obviously, Frederick Bernhardt died very young, sometime in mid-1864, and, Emilie, as a widow with a two-year-old child, could easily have remarried by the fall of that year.

Finally, the 1870 census for Missouri for Perry County, Brazeau Township, shows their only child Julia Reuschel but she was not with her parents. Instead, at age eight, she was living in a household headed by Henry Smith, who worked as a blacksmith, with his wife and children. She was the only person with that last name in the entire census. (Note that in 1860 the same Henry Smith household had no Reuschel living with them.) A good guess would be that Juliana was orphaned. With no death records available from the church for 1864 to 1876, the fates of Emilie (Siermann) Reuschel-Schuessler and her second husband Gottlieb will likely never be known. As noted above with the Koenig line, on April 24, 1884, Edward Koenig married Juliana Reuschel at the old wooden Immanuel Evangelical Lutheran Church in New Wells, Missouri. They had five children, and she lived until March 26, 1921.

On May 8, 2009, the steeple seen in the above photo for Trinity Lutheran Church was toppled by a storm with hundred-mile-per-hour winds. The church building dates to 1867, but the steeple was newer, perhaps twenty-years-old. A crane was brought in to remove the remnants that were "hanging by a thread" according to Chrystal Britt of KFVS Channel Twelve Heartland News. That same storm did considerable damage to the Kaempfe farm near Frohna.

CHAPTER NINE
DESCENDANTS OF ANDREAS KOENIG

1. Andreas KOENIG

sp: UNKNOWN

  2. Christian KOENIG (b.27 Sep 1799-Korbusssen,Thuringen,Germany;d.20 Aug 1877-Korbusssen,Thuringen,Germany)

    sp: Maria KIRMSE (b.8 Mar 1802-Muerken,Thuringen,Germany;m.13 Feb 1823;d.18 May 1865-Korbussen,Germany)

    3. Christina KOENIG (b.17 Oct 1823-Korbusssen,Thuringen,Germany;d.25 Nov 1918-Korbusssen,Germany)

      sp: Andreas HAERTLING (b.27 Mar 1805-Poeppeln,Germany;m.24 Nov 1844;d.30 Mar 1877-Poeppeln,Germany)

    3. Andreas KOENIG (b.12 Jul 1825-Korbussen,Saxe-Altenburg,Thuringia,Germany;d.13 Jan 1886-New Wells,MO)

      sp: Christina Justina HAERTLING (b.17Sep 1831-Poeppeln,Germany;m.26Mar1854;d.26Jul1890-New Wells, MO)

      4. Infant KOENIG (b.26 Nov 1854-Uniontown,Perry Co.,MO;d.26 Nov 1854-Uniontown,Perry Co.,MO)

      4. Eduard KOENIG (b.5 Apr 1856-Uniontown,Perry Co.,MO;d.10 Jan 1860-Frohna,Perry County,MO)

      4. Julius KOENIG (b.15 Oct 1857-Uniontown,Perry Co.,MO;d.17 May 1951-Pocahontas,CapeGirardeauCo.,MO)

        sp: Julie Elizabeth LOOS (b.abt 1859 ;m.22 Apr 1880)

        5. Alvine August or Nina KOENIG(*) (b.28 Aug 1883-New Wells,Cape Girardeau Co.,MO;d.19 Mar 1976)

        5. Wilhelm Edu. Friedr. KOENIG (b.Sep 1888;d.29 May 1890-New Wells,Cape Girardeau Co.,MO)

      4. Edward Wilhelm KOENIG (b.10 Jan 1861-Frohna,Perry Co.,MO;d.7 Sep 1944-Altenburg,Perry Co.,MO)

        sp: Juliana Mathilda REUSCHEL (b.1 Mar 1862-Wittenburg,MO;m.24 Apr 1884;d.26 Mar 1921-Perry Co., MO)

        5. Lina Christina KOENIG (b.15 Jan 1887-New Wells,MO;d.26 Dec 1955-Shrewsbury,St.Louis Co.,MO)

          sp: Theodor Samuel KAEMPFE (b.28 Jun 1882-Frohna,MO;m.8 Nov 1906;d.13 Dec 1963-CapeGir.,MO)

          6. Reinhold Albert KAEMPFE (b.6 Nov 1907-Frohna,Perry Co.,MO;d.5 Dec 1987-Frohna,Perry Co. MO)

            sp: Louisa SCHADE (b.26 Apr 1906;d.3 Feb 1999-St. Louis,MO)

            7. Wilma L. SCHADE (b.Abt Dec 1925-MO)

            7. LaVern SCHADE

            7. Delores M. SCHADE

              sp: Carl E. FADLER

          6. Paula Anita KAEMPFE (b.21 Jan 1910-Frohna,Perry Co.,MO;d.31 Jul 1995-Frohna,Perry Co. MO)

            sp: Alvin MEYER (b.2 Jun 1904;m.14 Apr 1940;d.May 1981)

            7. Imogene R. MEYER

              sp: Thomas "Jerry" J. UNGER

              8. Gregory UNGER

              8. Thomas UNGER

             7. Courtney MEYER

              sp: Connie KIRCHNER

              8. Caleb MEYER

              8. Joshua MEYER

              8. Anna MEYER

7. Marvis C. MEYER

sp: Sally A. LETTEER

7. Pearline MEYER

sp: Larry DEGENHARDT

8. Grant DEGENHARDT

8. Ryan DEGENHARDT

8. Tyler DEGENHARDT

8. Clay DEGENHARDT

7. Ritha C. MEYER

sp: Bruce G. HACKER

sp: Ernst W. VERSEMAN (b.14 Apr 1900-Perry Co.,MO;d.18 May 1998-Frohna,Perry Co. MO)

6. Alida Justine KAEMPFE (b.2 May 1913-Frohna,Perry Co.,MO;d.26 Dec 1995-Chesterfield,MO)

6. Raymond Hugo KAEMPFE (b.13 Sep 1917-Frohna,Perry Co.,MO;d.7 Jul 1971-Altenburg,Perry Co.,MO)

sp: Olga Sophia HAERTLING (b.27 Dec 1912-New Wells,MO;m.16Jan1944;d.30 Mar 1978-Altenburg,MO)

7. Betty Jean KAEMPFE

7. Faye Marie KAEMPFE (b.5 Feb 1949-New Wells,MO;d.7 Feb 1949-Cape Girardeau,MO)

6. Otto Harold KAEMPFE (b.14 Apr 1920-Frohna,Perry Co.,MO;d.29 May 1940-Frohna,Perry Co.,MO)

6. Elton Theobold KAEMPFE (b.15 Jul 1922-Frohna,Perry Co.,MO;d.26 Aug 1925-Frohna,Perry Co.,MO)

6. Milda Doris KAEMPFE (b.18 Mar 1925-Frohna,Perry Co.,MO;d.13 Apr 2008-St. Louis Co.,MO)

sp: Charles Joseph MONTI Sr. (b.28 Nov 1920-St. Louis,MO;m.6Jul1946;d.27 Jun 2006-St. Louis Co., MO)

7. Charles Joseph MONTI Jr.

sp: Vasana N. MALITONG-SIMON-CUNNINGHAM (m.17 Jul 1981)

8. May Lynn (Cunningham) MONTI (adopted)

7. Carmelo Louis MONTI AIA

sp: Mary Linda MILLER (m.1 Sep 1979)

8. Jason Miller MONTI

7. Michael James MONTI

sp: Mary POLITTE-MCGOWAN (m.17 Aug 1974(Div))

8. Candace Lee MONTI

8. Michelle (McGowan) MONTI (adopted)

8. Paul Michael (McGowan) MONTI (adopted)

7. Paul Stephen MONTI

sp: Ellen Marie VEIT (m.7 Aug 1976(Div))

8. Victoria Lynn MONTI

8. Stephen Paul MONTI

sp: Marsha Lynn SUMNER-REAGAN (m.23 Jun 1990)

8. Rebecca Lynn REAGAN

8. Isaac David REAGAN

8. Sarah Beth REAGAN

8. Jacob Warren REAGAN

7. Sheila Christine MONTI

  sp: Jose MOLINA (m.27 Dec 1985)

8. Molly MOLINA (stepdaughter)

7. Mark Edward MONTI

  sp: Kathleen A. SCANLON (b.7 Oct 1960;m.11 Feb 1984(Div);d.4 Feb 2008-Affton,St. Louis Co.,MO)

8. Christopher Joseph MONTI

8. Kayla Christine MONTI

  sp: Audra THOMAS (m.24 Apr 2007)

6. Regina Gladys KAEMPFE (b.7 Mar 1928-Frohna,Perry Co.,MO;d.12 Mar 1928-Frohna,Perry Co.,MO)

5. Eduard Kind neu KOENIG (b.Abt 1889;d.27 Sep 1889-New Wells,Cape Girardeau Co.,MO)

5. Esther Emilie KOENIG (b.13 Nov 1890-New Wells,Cape Girardeau Co.,MO)

5. Hilda KOENIG

5. Natalie L. KOENIG (b. 23 Aug 1896-Caldwell Co. ,MO; d. 21 Jan 1972-Perryville, Perry Co.,MO;

4. Maria Martha KOENIG (b.1 Nov 1862-Frohna,Perry Co.,MO;d.Aug. 30, 1874(*)-New Wells,Cape Gir. Co.,MO)

  sp: Herman KOENIG(*)

5. Emma Mathilda KOENIG(*) (b.22 Feb 1885-Saline Township,Perry Co.,MO)

4. Benjamin KOENIG (b.29 Nov 1864-Frohna,Perry Co.,MO;d.7 Dec 1959-Gordonville,Cape Girardeau Co.,MO)

  sp: Margaret KOLBE OR RUBSCH (b.abt.1867-New Wells,Cape Girardeau Co.,MO;m.28 Nov 1888)

5. Julius Herman KOENIG (b.31 Jan 1890-New Wells,Cape Girardeau Co.,MO;d.16 Jan 1894)

5. Bertha Marie KOENIG (b.8 Aug 1891-New Wells,Cape Girardeau Co.,MO)

5. Wm. Benjamen KOENIG

  sp: Louise Magde OBERNDORFER (m.7 Feb 1915)

4. Alwin "Alvin"J. KOENIG (b.30 Mar 1868-New Wells,Cape Girardeau Co.,MO;d.22 Feb 1940-New Wells,MO)

  sp: Martha A. SCHRUMPF (b.Abt 1871-Old Appleton,MO;m.11 Oct 1891;d.7 Nov 1893-New Wells,MO)

5. Flora Adeline KOENIG (b.25 Jan 1893-New Wells,Cape Girardeau Co.,MO;d.12 Jan 1978)

  sp: Otto Friedrich MEYR (b.2 Oct 1890-New Wells,Cape Girardeau Co.,MO;m.15 Feb 1914;d.10 Jan 1972)

6. Ruben MEYR (b.16 May 1915;d.3 Jul 1988)

  sp: Gertrude Alida SCHLIMPERT (b.1 Dec 1918;m.19 Feb 1939;d.1 Nov 2005)

7. Ryland Ruben "Dutch" MEYR (b.24 Jan 1940)

  sp: Joyce Karen MUELLER (b.15 Oct 1942;d.7 Feb 1998-St. Louis,MO)

8. Morgan Lynn MEYR

  sp: John Thadeus LAKE

  sp: Margaret Sharon MANNING (b.30 Aug 1946;d.2 Mar 2009)

8. Lindsey Michelle MEYR

7. Doris Emilie MEYR (b.3 Mar 1942;d.24 Nov 2006)

7. Larry Charles MEYR

7. Dennis Elroy MEYR

7. Glen Merlin MEYR

7. Loretta Jean MEYR

7. Rex Allen MEYR

6. Evelyn MEYR (b.19 Apr 1917;d.28 Oct 2004)

sp: Melvin HAERTLING

sp: Anna Elizabeth DIEFENBACH (b.12 Jul 1858;m.12 Feb 1896;d.3 Nov 1915-New Wells,Cape Gir. Co.,MO)

5. Ella KOENIG (b.Abt 1899)

sp: August LEIMBACH (b.Abt 1897)

6. Anita LEIMBACH (b.Abt 1920)

6. Milton LEIMBACH (b.Abt 1922)

6. Victoria LEIMBACH (b.Abt 1926)

4. Stillborn KOENIG (b.12 Oct 1871-New Wells,Cape Girardeau Co.,MO;d.12 Oct 1871-New Wells,MO)

3. Jacob KOENIG (b.28 Sep 1827-Korbusssen,Thuringen,Germany)

3. Justine KOENIG (b.3 Jul 1829-Korbussen,Ronneburg,Saxe-Altenburg,Germany)

sp: UNKNOWN

4. Sophie KOENIG (b.16 Dec 1848-Korbussen,Saxe-Altenburg,Germany;d.19 Feb 1921-New Wells,MO)

sp: Hermann HAERTLING (b.18 Jan 1841-Poeppeln,Germany;m.27 Dec 1866;d.13 Jul 1904-New Wells,MO)

5. Alvin Reinhold HAERTLING (b.1 Mar 1868-Shawneetown,Cape Girardeau Co.,MO;d.19 Mar 1947)

sp: Theresa WAGNER(*) (b.Abt. 1872-Shawneetown,Cape Girardeau Co.,MO)

6. Olga A. HAERTLING(*) (b.9 Nov 1899-Cape Girardeau Co.,MO;d.24 May 1937)

sp: Martin F. STIEMERS(*) (m.27 Nov 1927;d.11 Feb 1968)

5. Adolph Martin HAERTLING (b.18 Mar 1870-Shawneetown,Cape Gir.Co.,MO;d.28 Nov 1960-New Wells,MO)

sp: Martha (Meta) VOGTS (b.20Dec1870-Mersum,Hanover,Ger.;m.5Nov1891;d.14Feb1945-New Wells,MO)

6. Herman Benjamin HAERTLING(*) (b.10 Sep 1892-New Wells,Cape Girardeau Co.,MO;d.10 Apr 1970)

6. Otto W. HAERTLING(*) (b.31 Mar 1894-New Wells,Cape Girardeau Co.,MO;d.May 1984-St. Louis,MO)

6. Edmond Martin HAERTLING(*) (b.25 Mar 1900-New Wells,Cape Girardeau Co.,MO)

6. Ida Hedwig HAERTLING(*) (b.30 Jul 1902-New Wells,MO;d.9Nov 1978-Jackson,CapeGirardeauCo.,MO)

6. Infant HAERTLING(*) (b.Abt 1904-New Wells,Cape Girardeau Co.,MO;d.Abt 1904-New Wells,MO)

6. Adolph Martin HAERTLING (b.11 Feb 1911-New Wells,MO;d.13 Feb 1911-New Wells,MO)

6. Olga Sophia HAERTLING (b.27 Dec 1912-New Wells,MO;d.30 Mar 1978-Altenburg,Perry Co.,MO)

sp: Raymond Hugo KAEMPFE (b.13 Sep 1917-Frohna,MO;m.16 Jan 1944;d.7 Jul 1971-Altenburg,MO)

7. Betty Jean KAEMPFE (also on page 50)

7. Faye Marie KAEMPFE (also on page 50)

6. Living HAERTLING(*)

sp: Rudolph "Ben" MEYR(*) (b.26 Aug 1901-New Wells,Cape Girardeau Co.,MO)

5. Herman Oswald HAERTLING (b.4 Mar 1872-New Wells,Cape Girardeau Co.,MO;d.13 Sep 1940)

sp: Augusta E. PFEIFER (b.Abt 1876-Shawneetown,Cape Girardeau Co.,MO;m.5 Jul 1896;d.9 Sep 1956)

  6. Charles A. HAERTLING AIA (b.21 Oct 1928-St. Genevieve,MO;d.20 Apr 1984-Boulder,CO)

  6. Alfons Elmer HAERTLING (b.1 May 1908-Cape Girardeau Co.,MO;d.17 Nov 1957-Apple Creek,MO)

  6. Erwin Florence HAERTLING (b.19 Mar 1910-New Wells,MO;d.5 Mar 1911-New Wells,MO)

5. Julius Paul HAERTLING (b.27 Apr 1874-New Wells,MO;d.18 Jul 1966-Perryville,Perry Co.,MO)

  sp: Magdalene Lina STARZINGER(b.11Jun1877-NewWells,MO;m.26Dec1897;d.20Oct1951-Pocahontas,MO)

  6. Friedrich Paul HAERTLING (b.5 Nov 1898-New Wells,,MO;d.4 Jan 1972-Pocahantos,CapeGir.Co.MO)

    sp: RosaElizabethAnnaRICHTER(b.26Aug1900-Wittenberg,MO;m.14Nov1920;d.10Jan1989-CapeGir.,MO)

    7. Mildred Helen HAERTLING

     sp: Sylvester Roger LOAR (m.29 Mar 1947)

     sp: Gene Edward MILLER

    7. Melbert Ralph HAERTLING

     sp: Mary Lou MACKE (m.22 Jan 1950)

    7. Nelson Arthur HAERTLING

     sp: Melba Clare SEATON (b.21 Jan 1941-Miami,OK;m.12 Sep 1964;d.2 Aug 2006-Bastrop,TX)

     8. Andrea Gail HAERTLING

     8. Teresa Lynn HAERTLING

      sp: William Kurt TAEGER (m.20 Feb 1993)

    7. Allen Leroy HAERTLING

     sp: Betty Jane CHANDLER (m.27 Dec 1964)

  6. Walter Hermann HAERTLING (b.3 Jun 1901-New Wells,Cape Girardeau Co.,MO;d.25 May 1968-IL)

    sp: Frieda L. BODENSHATZ (b. 21 Dec 1904;m.6 Sep 1925; d. 25 May 1968)

  6. Wilma Anita HAERTLING (b.19 Oct 1903-New Wells,CapeGirardeauCo.,MO;d.27 Oct 1985-St.Louis,MO)

    sp: Ralph SMITH

  6. Elsa Emma HAERTLING (b.9 Jun 1906-New Wells,CapeGirardeauCo.,MO;d.13 Feb 2003-Kingston,NY)

    sp: August NOELKER (m.(Div))

    sp: Edward STOLL

  6. Lydia Lynn HAERTLING (b.12 Mar 1909-New Wells,CapeGirardeauCo.,MO;d.14 Apr 1983-Frohna,MO)

    sp: Otis MILSTER

  6. Hilda Louise HAERTLING (b.11 Apr 1914-New Wells,Cape Girardeau Co.,MO)

    sp: Raymond SEXTON

  6. Elmer Roland HAERTLING (b.25 Sep 1916-New Wells,CapeGirardeauCo.,MO;d.18 Feb 1982-CA)

    sp: Bernice DAY

5. Gustav Herman HAERTLING (b.8 May 1876-Shawneetown,CapeGirardeauCo.,MO;d.1Jul1959-St.Louis,MO)

  sp: Louise KOENIG (b.abt 1880;m.16 Jun 1901)

5. Fredrich Wilhelm HAERTLING(*) (b.23 Mar 1879-Shawneetown,Cape Girardeau Co.,MO;d.7 Jul 1962)

    sp: Agnas JAHN(*) (b.Abt 1883-Shawneetown,Cape Girardeau Co.,MO;m.7 Jul 1902)

5. Amalie Lina HAERTLING(*) (b.14 Jun 1882-Shawneetown,Cape Girardeau Co.,MO;d.11 Mar 1922)

    sp: Fred BREMER(*) (b.Abt 1878-Shawneetown,Cape Girardeau Co.,MO;m.27 Jul 1902)

5. Benjamin Arno HAERTLING (b.22 Dec 1884-New Wells,MO;d.29 Jan 1957-Cape Girardeau,MO)

    sp: Ida GERHARTER (b.11 Dec 1883-Shawneetown,MO;m.3 May 1908;d.Oct 1978-Jackson,MO)

5. Bertha Louise HAERTLING (b.9 Jul 1888-Shawneetown,Cape Girardeau Co.,MO;d.24 May 1976)

    sp: August M. MEYR (b.1 Sep 1887-Shawneetown,MO;d.28 Jan 1928-Cape Girardeau Co.,MO)

5. Infant HAERTLING (b.9 Jul 1888-Shawneetown,Cape Girardeau Co.,MO)

3. Zacharius KOENIG (b.9 Oct 1830-Korbusssen,Thuringen,Germany;d.9 Dec 1908-Pocahontas,CapeGir.Co.,MO)

3. Marie KOENIG (b.13 Jun 1832-Korbusssen,Thuringen,Germany;d.27 Sep 1832-Korbusssen,Germany)

3. Christian KOENIG (b.2 Jan 1834-Korbusssen,Thuringen,Germany)

3. Georg KOENIG (b.25 Feb 1835-Korbusssen,Thuringen,Germany)

3. Gottfried KOENIG (b.23 Oct 1836-Korbusssen,Thuringen,Germany;d.1 Nov 1836-Korbusssen,Germany)

3. Valenin KOENIG (b.10 Jan 1838-Korbusssen,Thuringen,Germany)

3. Maria KOENIG (b.10 Aug 1839-Korbusssen,Thuringen,Germany;d.6 Oct 1839-Korbusssen,Germany)

3. Eva KOENIG (b.12 Oct 1840-Korbusssen,Thuringen,Germany;d.20 Jun 1858)

3. Herman KOENIG (b.7 Mar 1843-Korbusssen,Thuringen,Germany;d.30 Apr 1869-New Wells,CapeGir.Co.,MO)

3. Stillborn KOENIG (b.5 Oct 1844-Korbusssen,Thuringen,Germany;d.5 Oct 1844-Korbusssen,Germany)

3. Pauline KOENIG (b.21 Feb 1848-Korbusssen,Thuringen,Germany)

Four Generations of Koenig Descendants
Circa Summer 1944
Seated: Edward Wilhelm Koenig
Standing, Left to Right: Lina (Koenig) Kaempfe and Paula (Kaempfe) Meyer holding baby Imogene Meyer.
Photo courtesy of Imogene (Meyer) Unger

CHAPTER TEN

DESCENDANTS OF JOHANN HAERTLING

1. Johann HAERTLING (b.19 Sep 1776-Korbusssen,Germany;d.3 Feb 1841-Poeppeln,Germany)

  sp: Regina NUENDEL (b.24 Aug 1779-Poeppeln,Germany;m.8 Jul 1800;d.18 Apr 1845-Poeppeln,Germany)

    2. Andreas HAERTLING (b.27 Mar 1805-Poeppeln,Thuringen,Germany;d.30 Mar 1877-Poeppeln,Germany)

      sp: Maria ALBRECHT (b.Abt 1809-Baldenhain,Germany;m.26 Apr 1831;d.15 May 1844-Poeppeln,Germany)

      3. Christina Justina HAERTLING (b.17 Sep 1831-Poeppeln,Thuringia,Germany;d.26 Jul 1890-New Wells,MO)

        sp: Andreas KOENIG (b.12 Jul 1825-Korbussen,Germany;m.21 Mar 1854;d.13 Jan 1886-New Wells,MO)

For descendants of Christina Justina Haertling and Andreas Koenig see Chapter Nine, pages 49-54

      3. Maria HAERTLING (b.1 Jun 1833-Poeppeln,Altenburg,Germany;d.13 Feb 1899-New Wells,Cape Gir. Co.,MO)

        sp: Gottfried KOCH (b.3 Apr 1827-Korbussne,Germany;m.15 Sep 1854;d.8 Oct 1870-New Wells,MO)

        4. Pauline KOCH (b.12 Dec 1855-Altenburg, Perry Co.,MO;d.14 Jan 1925-New Wells, Cape Girardeau Co.,MO)

        4. Jacob KOCH (b.14 Mar 1857-Altenburg, Perry Co.,MO;d.8 Sep 1931-New Wells, Cape Girardeau Co.,MO)

        4. Friedrich Edward KOCH (b.17 Feb 1860-New Wells, Cape Girardeau Co., MO; d.15 Feb 1938-New Wells,MO)

        4. Julius Emil KOCH (b.4 Feb 1863-New Wells, Cape Girardeau Co.,MO)

        4. Hermann Martin KOCH (b.14 Feb 1869-New Wells,Cape Girardeau Co.,MO;d.19 Aug 1921-New Wells,MO)

          sp: Friedrich JAHN (m.20 May 1879)

      3. Georg HAERTLING (b.13 Oct 1835-Poeppeln,Thuringen,Germany;d.17 Dec 1860-Poeppeln,Germany)

      3. Hermann HAERTLING (b.6 Jan 1838-Poeppeln,Thuringen,Germany;d.16 Feb 1840-Poeppeln,Germany)

      3. Friedrich Heinrich HAERTLING (b.28 Jan 1840-Poeppeln,Germany;d.31 Jan 1840-Poeppeln,Germany)

      3. Hermann HAERTLING (b.18 Jan 1841-Poeppeln,Altenburg,Germany;d.13 Jul 1904-New Wells,MO)

        sp: Sophie KOENIG (b.16 Dec1848-Korbussen,Germany;m.27 Dec1866;d.19 Feb1921-New Wells,,MO)

For descendants of Hermann Haertling and Sophie Koenig, see Chapter Nine, pages 52-54

      3. Pauline HAERTLING (b.14 Aug 1842-Poeppeln,Thuringen,Germany;d.4 Sep 1842)

      3. Johanna Pauline HAERTLING (b.20 Dec 1843-Poeppeln,Germany;d.25 Apr 1863-Poeppeln,Germany)

  sp: Christina KOENIG (b.17 Oct 1823-K,Germany;m.24 Nov 1844;d.25 Nov 1918-Korbusssen,Germany)

    2. Regiena HAERTLING

    2. Maria HAERTLING

    2. Rosina HAERTLING (b.17 Apr 1809-Poeppeln,Thuringen,Germany)

- 2. Gottfried HAERTLING (b.24 Nov 1811-Poeppeln, Thuringen,Germany;d.10 Jan 1814-Poeppeln,Germany)
- 2. Christian HAERTLING (b.7 Apr 1814-Poeppeln,Thuringen,Germany;d.6 Nov 1864-Poeppeln,Germany)
- 2. Justina HAERTLING (b.23 May 1816-Poeppeln,Thuringen,Germany)
- 2. Stillborn HAERTLING (b.1 Aug 1818-Poeppeln,Thuringen,Germany;d.1 Aug 1818-Poeppeln,Germany)
- 2. Christina HAERTLING (b.12 Dec 1819-Poeppeln,Thuringen,Germany;d.25 Aug 1821-Poeppeln,Germany)
- 2. Christina HAERTLING (b.19 Apr 1822)

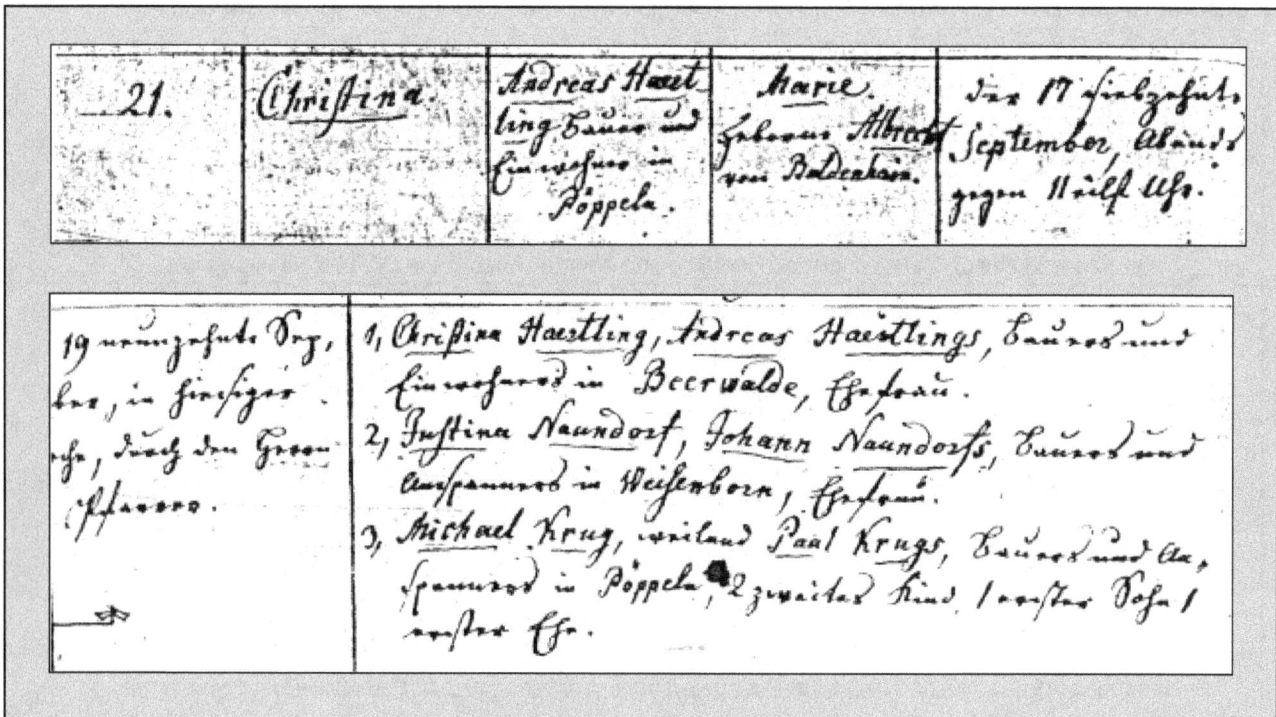

Birth Record for Christina Haertling
From: Lutheran Church records for 1831, Korbussen, Germany
Line 21 in the book shows Christina born to Andreas Heartling from Poeppeln and his wife
Marie nee Albrecht from Baldenhain on the 17th day of September. She was baptized on the 19th.
Image courtesy of Nelson A. Haertling

Lutheran Church in Korbussen, Germany
Ink rendering by Carmelo L. Monti

Aerial View of the Farm Near Frohna, Missouri
Circa 1962
Photo courtesy of Miller-Monti Collection

PART THREE

A FARM NEAR FROHNA

Century Farm Award Logo

The University of Missouri Century Farm Award, jointly sponsored by the University's Extension program; MU College of Agriculture, Food and Natural Resources; and the Missouri Farm Bureau
Image courtesy of University of Missouri Extension Publications

Three Kaempfe - Koenig Generations
Circa Summer 1916
Photo courtesy of Milda (Kaempfe) Monti Estate

Back row, standing, left to right: Justine (Hennecke) Kaempfe, Esther (Koenig) Ernst holding her son Alfred Ernst, Juliana (Reuschel) Koenig, Lina (Koenig) Kaempfe, Hilda (Koenig) Rabold, and Natalia (Koenig) Kasten.

Front row: Theodor S. Kaempfe (kneeling), Alida Kaempfe, Reinhold A. Kaempfe, Paula Kaempfe and Edward Koenig (seated).

Note that Edward and Juliana (Reuschel) Koenig were the parents of these four sisters: Lina, Esther, Hilda, and Natalie. Justine (Hennecke) Kaempfe was Theodor's mother. Theodor and Lina (Koenig) Kaempfe were the parents of Alida, Reinhold, and Paula.

MISSOURI
CENTURY
FARM

A program of
University of Missouri Extension and the
MU College of Agriculture, Food and Natural Resources

CHAPTER ELEVEN

GROWING UP ON A FARM NEAR FROHNA

Theodor Samuel Kaempfe grew up on the farm west of Frohna that his father Traugott Gotthilf Kaempfe purchased in 1876 from Robert M. Smith. The original farm consisted of 11.6 acres in one section and 91.6 acres in another. Theodor married Lina Christina Koenig from New Wells, Cape Girardeau County, Missouri, in 1906, and, as the youngest son remaining at home, he and his bride probably stayed there to help his parents. After Traugott died in 1909, his wife Justine and probably all eight of their children inherited the farm. In 1912, Theodor bought out the other heirs and later purchased parcels of land from neighbors, expanding the farm's size to 132 acres. (See the USGS Map Altenburg Quadrangle 1949 on page 26.)

Together, Lina and Theodor expanded the lovely homestead to include plentiful fruit trees, fishing ponds, pastures and plowed fields, with flower gardens surrounding a nice, comfortable white frame house with a wide front porch, wood siding and a metal gabled roof. Other buildings included a large horse, mule, and cow barn; several equipment sheds for wagons and plows; garage for the buggy; chicken coop; hog barn with adjacent pens; feed silos; wood shed; and outhouses, since they had no indoor plumbing. Water was drawn from a cistern.

Kaempfe Farm House near Frohna, Missouri
Lina Kaempfe with unknown guest and a cat
Photo courtesy of Imogene (Meyer) Unger

They built Purple Martin houses on tall poles to attract the bug-eating swallows, kept a canary in a cage inside the house, and had many cats.

Between 1907 and 1928, the couple parented eight children, all born at home with the help of midwives, all christened in their first days of life at Concordia Lutheran Church, first established in 1839, where the family attended church every Sunday morning. Although they were third generation Americans, they and many of the people of the region were still ethnically pure German and still spoke the language as their native tongue. Several grandchildren, who spent summers either visiting or working on the farm during the 1950s, report that they learned German by listening to conversations between their grandparents, parents, aunts, and uncles.

On March 18, 1925 the Great Tornado roared through their surrounding community around 2:00 p.m. The funnel cloud was nearly a mile wide and stayed on the ground for two

Cleanup After the Great Tornado of March 18, 1925
Photo dated March 25, 1925 courtesy of Imogene (Meyer) Unger

hundred nineteen miles, traveling from Ellington, Missouri into Indiana and setting records that have never been broken. Estimates for the dead exceed 800, with nearly 3,000 injured and 15,000 homes destroyed. At least three towns were completely demolished. Among the dead was Martha Helene (Gemeinhardt) Kaempfe (Theodor's widowed sister-in-law) who died instantly from a broken neck. His sister Louise Wilhelmine (Kaempfe) Stueve received fatal, internal injuries and died ten days later. Theodor's wife Lina was pregnant with her seventh child and she gave birth prematurely that day to Milda Doris Kaempfe.

Five months later their three-year-old youngest son Elton died from meningitis. In September Theodor's widowed mother Justine (Hennecke) Kaempfe, who had lived on the farm for nearly forty-nine years—the last seven as an invalid after having a stroke—died in their home. With the happy exception of Milda's birth, those six months in 1925 surely stand as the worst period in the history of the Kaempfe family, perhaps closely matched only by the sixteen-month period of April 1847 to August 1848 when Juliane (Lippisch) Kaempfe and three of her children died in St. Louis.

In 1928, Theodor and Lina's last child to be born, Regina, died within a matter of days of birth, leaving six surviving siblings who grew to adulthood, and, finally, life began to improve for the family. During the Great Depression, they were able to keep the farm; homegrown food was plentiful; but they felt the lean times and did without things they formerly had purchased, like sugar, coffee, and new clothes. Instead they worked hard and ate the fruits of their labor. Theodor had vineyards and produced three varieties of homemade sweet wines; he made apple cider in the fall; and they brewed root beer. In the summertime they picked blackberries, boysenberries and red raspberries. Other fruit included Jonathan apples, cherries, peaches, persimmons, sour "sweet" apples, and two kinds of pears. In a big garden near the house, they sometimes grew strawberries, watermelons, and cantaloupes, but they always planted potatoes, carrots, celery, onions, peas, a variety of beans, and cabbage to make sauerkraut. They tended an herb garden. Black walnut trees, which grew naturally all over the farm, produced nuts inside big green husks and dense, rock-hard shells that required a hammer to break. The children gathered eggs twice a day from the chicken coop and if there were too many they were sold to the market in town. Meowmey, a barnyard cat that was a favorite in later years with the grandchildren, had her ears pecked off by the chickens, but another cat, Whitey, was Lina's favorite and was the only cat allowed in the house.

Theodor Kaempfe with his Hounds
On the farm west of Frohna, Missouri
Photo courtesy of Milda (Kaempfe) Monti Estate

Chickens were occasionally killed for dinner—an unpleasant task requiring a chopping block; plucking the feathers was a nasty job that no one wanted. Cows were kept mainly for the dairy products, but occasionally one was butchered for the beef. Theodor was known for his veterinary skills and was called upon by many neighbors to help "pull a calf." Pigs were slaughtered when they wanted to make pork sausage or smoke hams and bacon. Animal fat was rendered to make soap. Ponds were stocked with catfish, and all summer long children went fishing. During hunting season, Theodor pulled out a twelve-gauge double-barreled shotgun to hunt squirrels and rabbits, with Trixie and Tiny (rat terrier dogs) flushing out the prey. He was fond of fox and coon hunting and kept half-a-dozen hounds on the farm for that purpose. On Christmas Day, after a big noontime feast, the dogs were let loose and everyone went hunting rabbits and quail. They used a "22" to kill owls or hawks that swooped down to steal chickens, an occasional snake in the field, or frogs from the pond (hunted at night) for fixing frog leg dinners. An air rifle was suitable for target practice and to instill safe handling, and most of the children became excellent marksmen, even the girls. Milda was particularly good, but Raymond was perhaps the best "shot-gunner," especially when quail hunting—he readily shot them in flight.

Paula (Kaempfe) Meyer-Verseman recalled her childhood on the farm when she wrote an autobiographical essay in March 1990. The children had chores to do and one of hers was "to turn the cows out after we were done milking and one turned around and (stepped) on my little toe and almost cut it off, but dad said just thank the Lord its not all the way off—you still have it yet." Another time, after throwing hay from the second floor to the first floor, she jumped down onto the hay pile and landed on a concealed pitchfork. One prong "went through my right leg and busted the skin wide open and dad said just be thankful it did not go through your stomach." Theodor told her to "thank the Lord—we must go through much suffering, for all the sins we do, but we ask him to heal us and bear our pain."

Both Paula and her sister Milda recalled another frightening experience. When the family went to New Wells to visit Lina's family, they piled into a horse-drawn buggy and headed south, past Rudy Hellweg's home. At Apple Creek, which is the border between Perry and Cape Girardeau Counties, their parents warned them to "hold on to whatever you can so you don't fall out and drown," as they went down the steep side of the creek's embankment—no one ever did.

Lunchtime in the Wheat Field at Harvest Time c. 1936
Lina (Koenig) Kaempfe provided a picnic lunch to neighbor Walter Wenger (far left), her husband Theodor Kaempfe (far right), and their two sons Otto (top center) and Reinhold (right center). Notice the wheat stacks in the background.
Photo courtesy of Miller-Monti Collection

Theodor's favorite horses were Doc and June, and he hitched them to a wagon to drive into Frohna to buy household supplies like flour at the mill, taking along grandchildren in the summer. He did not own an automobile for many years, but in the 1950s he finally decided to learn to drive and bought a black 1949 Plymouth. In the spring neighboring families helped each other out by working communally to plow each other's fields. Theodor tilled the fields by using a plow pulled by a team of mules. He had a four-blade plow with wheels lined up at each end of the blades and a seat above the carriage that held the blades together—probably a John Deere Gilpin Two-Wheel Sulky model. The mules were hitched up front and they took several days to till his acreage, even though portions of the land lay fallow each year in

Theodor Kaempfe with his "Dear John" Tractor
Photo courtesy of Imogene (Meyer) Unger

rotation to prevent depletion of nutrients. They grew clover then turned it under so the nitrogen would enrich the soil for the following year. They planted wheat, corn, barley, cotton, and soybeans. In later years as his health declined and his son Ramey came to help work the farm, Theodor decided to buy a John Deere B tractor, which he himself never operated.

Imogene (Meyer) Unger, a granddaughter who grew up in Frohna, described cherry picking time that began at the end of the school year. "We were given a large wire hook which we used to pull the branches toward us so we could reach the cherries. We would climb up in the tree or use a ladder." Her brother Courtney Meyer described how he and his brother Marvis "stomped hay" during the summer as it was tossed into the wagon and they earned five-cents a load, perhaps as much as twenty-cents a day. In the middle of summer, "threshing ring meetings" were held at the farm "since it was the central location to all the neighbors who participated. . . . (they) would plan the schedule." The community worked together again at the end of summer for the harvest. A threshing machine was brought in and each farm took about two days of work. Courtney, who was too young to pitch bundles into the wagon, served as a waterboy. The farmers' wives came together and prepared lunches that they delivered to the men, who were hauling wheat shocks to the threshing machine in the barnyard. By the end of the day after many wagonloads had been emptied, an enormous haystack was mounded high in the air and the wheat was carried to the granary for storage. About six farmers participated and after the work was completed all around, Theodor had all the families over to his farm so they could "settle up" their fence rail issues. The event was more like a party since "Grampa was always a good host and he did enjoy entertaining his friends."

Lina Kaempfe with her Cats
Notice the grape arbor alongside the house
Photo courtesy of Imogene (Meyer) Unger

While the family began farm chores early in the morning at dawn, Lina and some of the girls cooked up a big breakfast of sausage and bacon with eggs and pancakes or biscuits on the wood-burning stove in the kitchen. Then she rang the dinner bell so everyone stopped their chores and walked to the house. After cleaning up the dishes, she made sugar cookies to keep on hand for children who stopped by on their way home from school. Dog food was made from scratch by mixing ground corn and grease, among other things, and the dough was baked so that "it smelled good enough to eat." The sour "sweet" apples were baked into hearty, delicious pies. Laundry was done in a big galvanized tub by scrubbing the clothes on a serrated metal washboard, wringing them out with a hand-crank wringer, and hanging to dry on lines outside. Lina tended the vegetable garden at the rear of the house and planted flowers in the yard. Perennials included hibiscus, crepe myrtle trees, and at least a dozen rose bushes. Flowers included day lilies, irises, marigolds, daisies, Black-eyed Susans, carnations, and many different colors of snapdragons, which the grandchildren loved to squeeze and pinch open. She was the primary caregiver to her mother-in-law Justine, who was an invalid from 1918 to 1925. After cooking lunch and dinner, darning and mending were done to keep clothing usable, and when a piece was beyond repair, it was used for rags or to make quilts or blankets, which the wives of the community did as a group activity. Nothing was wasted.

The children walked two-and-a-half miles each way to elementary school in Frohna, where they learned German as their first language and then English. When it came time for high school not all of them were able to go, as this required finding transportation to Brazeau, about eight miles away and too far to walk. Milda, as the youngest child, was one of the lucky ones.

New tragedies befell the family. Alida, their middle daughter, had always been moody; as a young woman she began to display symptoms of depression and violence towards her mother and by 1934 required hospitalization. In 1940, their youngest son Otto fell to his death while painting the roof of the "feedmill." Raymond was inducted into the Army during World War Two, and soon three other children left to seek opportunity in the big city.

Despite these separations, the family remained close. Raymond returned to the area after the war, married and began farming in New Wells. After living in St. Louis for a while, Paula returned to Frohna, became the town's telephone operator, and bought a house. She married and raised her family there. Reinhold moved to St. Louis but kept hounds on the farm. Milda also lived in St. Louis, but returned each summer. Her first and second sons Charles and Carmelo Monti were baptized together in Frohna Lutheran Church. The collection of portraits of each sibling from that generation, found in Chapter Twelve, illustrates the Kaempfe family's continued assimilation into the broader American culture, even while the allure of the family farm called them home.

Kaempfe Family Reunion
Autumn 1947
Photo courtesy of Imogene (Meyer) Unger

Theodor Samuel and Lina Christina (Koenig) Kaempfe
40th Wedding Anniversary November 8, 1946
Photo courtesy of Milda (Kaempfe) Monti Estate

Family of Theodor and Lina (Koenig) Kaempfe
Top: circa 1931 (25th wedding anniversary)
Left to Right: Otto, Raymond, Reinhold, Lina, Milda, Theodor, Paula and Alida
Bottom: March 1937
Left to Right: Raymond, Paula, Theodor, Lina, Milda, Reinhold, and Otto
Photos courtesy of Imogene (Meyer) Unger

CHAPTER TWELVE

PORTRAITS OF EIGHT KAEMPFE SIBLINGS

Reinhold Albert Kaempfe *(November 6, 1907—December 5, 1987)*

Reinhold (Reiney) was christened on November 17, 1907, when he was eleven days old. He appeared in the 1910 Missouri census as Reinhold A., a two-year-old grandson of Justine Kaempfe, a widow who owned her farm. Her son Theodor S. and his wife Lina C. lived with her. By the 1920 Missouri census Reinhold was twelve, lived with his parents Theodore (*sic*) S. and Lena (*sic*) C., and worked as a farm laborer on his home farm. Justine lived with them but

was no longer the head-of-household. By age twenty-two in 1930, Reiney apparently struck out on his own, as he was working as a farm laborer in Cuming County, Nebraska for a family headed by Casper Hoegemeyer. By December 1948 he was back in Missouri, as he agreed to be godfather to Milda's son Charles Monti Jr. when he was christened in Frohna at Concordia Lutheran Church.

Around 1945 to 1950, he married Louisa Schade who already had two young teenage daughters, Delores and LaVern, from her first marriage to Rudolph H. Schade, a farmer from Frohna who died tragically at age forty-seven in February 1943. Rudolph's parents Ernst and Mary Schade owned the farm up the road from the Kaempfe farm, so if newly-widowed Louisa lived with her in-laws after her husband's death, perhaps that was how she and Reiney became acquainted. Reiney helped to raise the girls, but Louisa was already close to forty years old so they never had any children together. Charles Monti Sr., his sister Milda's husband, helped Reiney get a Union job at the American Can Company in St. Louis after the war at a time when jobs

Courtesy of Milda (Kaempfe) Monti Estate

were scarce. He worked as an oilier and machinist maintenance worker during the third shift until his retirement and always expressed gratitude to Charlie for that favor. His family moved and they bought a house on Lansdowne Avenue in the city just east of McCausland. Louisa went to work as a cleaning lady at some of the well-to-do apartments located in South St. Louis.

Soon after starting to work Reiney was able to afford his own car. Over the years he owned a distinctive pink-and-black Chrysler Desoto, a 1955 red Ford two-door, and a tan Dodge that he bought near retirement.

Reiney enjoyed playing the card game Pinochle with his brother Ramey and brothers-in-law, and in St. Louis, he and Louisa played with Milda and Charlie. His nephew Carmelo Monti said that when his parents went to visit Uncle Reiney and Aunt Louisa during the 1950s, he and his brothers took some board games along because Louisa's daughters were already grown and gone and there was nothing for the boys to do in her extremely neat, well-kept house. The grownups played cards and the kids stayed in the living room entertaining each other, and generally they got very bored, but Reiney was known for his story telling and so he kept everyone amused. Another nephew Courtney Meyer recalled rooming with Reiney and Louisa for three summers while he worked at the American Can Company to pay for college.

Reinhold Kaempfe on Main Street in Frohna, Missouri
Buildings to the left: Bank and grocery store
Building to the right (foreground): Bowling alley/antique shop
Photo courtesy of Milda (Kaempfe) Monti Estate

During all the years that he worked in St. Louis, Reiney hoped to return to Frohna and take over his parents' farm, a dream that went unfulfilled. He bought hounds in the late 1950's and kept them briefly in the care of his father at the farm where he loved to go out hunting. Finally, late in life Reiney moved back to Frohna without Louisa—she chose to stay in the city—but they remained amicable and never divorced. Sometime during the late 1970s he entered politics, running as "R. A. Kaempfe" for "Democratic Candidate for Commissioner for Eastern District of Perry County, Missouri." A poster with his photo reads, "Vote for R. A. Kaempfe," and, "Your vote and influence will be appreciated." He did not win the election.

In Frohna, he lived in a trailer next door to his sister Paula's house. Although Paula provided meals for him, he tended a garden across the street behind the bowling alley. Since he was well up into his seventies with bad knees, crossing the street was a bit of a chore, so the town of Frohna erected a yellow highway pedestrian-crossing sign for him, and everyone joked that it should read, "Reiney Crossing." (Some swear that it did.) He was eighty years old when he died in 1987, and Louisa lived until 1999. He is buried in Concordia Lutheran Cemetery in Frohna and leaves behind two stepdaughters and their families.

Paula Anita (Kaempfe) Meyer-Verseman *(January 21, 1910—July 31, 1995)*

Paula was christened on January 30, 1910 when she was nine days old. She appeared as a two-month-old in 1910 and at age eleven in 1920 with her parents in Missouri censuses. In her autobiographical essay that she wrote in March 1990 she recalled that her grandmother Justine (Hennecke) Kaempfe had a stoke (around 1918), was bedridden and paralyzed, and one of Paula's duties as the oldest daughter was to stay home and take care of her grandmother on Sundays while the rest of the family went to church. She attended elementary school but not high school, as the family could not afford to send her. Instead, at age thirteen, she went to work for some wealthier families, first in Brazeau, then during her later teen years in St. Louis where she worked as a cook. In the 1930 St. Louis census, Paula is shown as a twenty-year-old maid working for Myron and Florence Stuetevant in their rented apartment located in the Greystone Apartment Building at 4397 McPherson. He was a banker from Massachusetts. Lawyers, accountants, professors, and a newspaper editor occupied other units and most had maids or cooks living in their households.

In 1939 she returned to Frohna on a vacation while her parents were building an addition to their house. Alvin Meyer from Farrar, Missouri was a carpenter; his crew was doing the work. Paula learned of a job opening as a telephone switchboard operator, so she took the job and did not return to St. Louis. She was able to buy the little brick house in town where the switchboard equipment was located from her cousin. After she married Alvin on April 14, 1940, he moved into her house and remodeled and updated it by adding indoor plumbing and hot water. The

Photo courtesy of Imogene (Meyer) Unger

operator job kept Paula tied down, she wrote, as she connected calls night and day, with Sunday mornings for church services her only time off, but she held the job for a number of years.

Over the course of their lives, Paula and Alvin were quite entrepreneurial and managed a variety of businesses. They purchased the white-frame building across the street, originally built in the 1830s by August Lueders and later used by his son Paul as a photography studio and a barbershop. Alvin had taken correspondence courses in taxidermy through a school in Omaha, Nebraska, and he was licensed in 1930, so he converted the building with its big skylight into the office for his carpentry business and his taxidermy shop, which was a successful part-time job for many years. Alvin's brother's Bill, Rudy and Fritz Meyer suggested that Frohna needed some entertainment, so the four brothers formed the Meyer Development Company and bought another Lueders' property called the Wine Cellar or the Lueders Store, where the old-timers had stored the family's wine produced from a large vineyard, and there they built a four-lane bowling alley in 1954. Alvin was always handy in construction, a carpenter by trade, having built a number of houses and barns with large round-top roofs in the area, so he converted the second

Paula Kaempfe and Alvin Meyer
Married April 14, 1940
Accompanying the bride and groom were two flower girls (Millie Meyer and Arlene Kaempfe), four bridesmaids, four groomsmen, and one ring bearer.
Photo courtesy of Milda (Kaempfe) Monti Estate

floor of the bowling alley building into three apartments that could be rented out. Paula did the cleaning, kept the books for the bowling alley, and managed the apartments. Their daughter Imogene (Meyer) Unger wrote, "Alvin spent every night at the lanes while the bowlers were there, keeping up with the boys who set pins, renting shoes, and (running) the snack bar." Alvin died in 1981 and Paula continued to manage the lanes until they closed in 1984. Paula wrote, "We were really thankful to all the nice people that came from different towns for our business."

During this time they had five children and Paula was godmother to Milda's first-born son Charles Monti Jr. She seemed to have endless energy and was always baking cakes, pies, coffee cake, and strudel as well as preparing large meals for all of her guests, including her brother Reiney after he moved back to Frohna. They had several acres of land behind the building where they kept a garden. Paula spent days in the kitchen canning the fruits and vegetables they harvested, and Imogene recalled that pulling weeds in the garden was quite the chore. She took care of chickens and sheep while Alvin kept a few hogs and a cow that he milked everyday before work, then separated the cream. They held an annual butchering event at their house, and Theodor and Raymond were known to make the best sausage.

The children came home from Concordia Lutheran School for lunch during nice weather, and the house was the gathering place for all of the town's children. In the winter when it snowed, they went to Meyer's Hill for sleigh riding; in summer there were baseball games at a ballpark in town. Saturday was bath and hair-wash night—even Lina came into town so Imogene could roll up her hair—and on Sunday morning everyone went to church at Concordia Lutheran.

When her children were grown, Paula was proud of their accomplishments and was happy that she had been able to help many of them open their own businesses with cash or loans or was able to see them go to college. After the bowling alley closed, she managed the apartments until 1989, but finally sold the building to Imogene who converted the main floor into a successful antique shop, which she operated until 2005. Paula's son Courtney Meyer wrote, "One of the great servant efforts of Paula was to care for the elderly in her own home. Her dream was to have a nursing home. That never materialized but somewhere between fifteen and twenty elderly were lovingly cared for by Paula during their final years of life. All were invited if able to eat all their meals with the Meyer family."

Paula knew Ernst Verseman, an old friend and a widower who lived near Theodor's farm, and he came to help her. They surprised nearly everyone in the family with their "September romance" as they married in April 1987 (Courtney was the best man), and Ernst moved into town into her house. Not long after the wedding, she suffered a series of strokes that left her unable to walk. After physical therapy, she regained sufficient use of her hands so she was able to braid rugs and small baskets, sew blankets for Lutheran World Relief, and make quilts from her own designs, which she quilted on her old sewing machine. Ever the optimist, she entered contests and won some money once, enough she thought to buy a new Singer should her old one break. She expressed the hope that the young people of Frohna would get to work and preserve the old buildings of the town by finding new uses for them—something she and Alvin had done. She and Ernst lived together for five years, but eventually, she became incapacitated and moved into a nursing home in Perryville. In 1995 she suffered a final massive stroke and died on July 31st at age eighty-five. She is buried in Concordia Lutheran Cemetery in Frohna, and is survived by five children, nine grandchildren, and nine great-grandchildren.

Alida Justine Kaempfe *(May 2, 1913—December 26, 1995)*

Alida was christened on May 11, 1913 when she was nine days old. She appears at age six and sixteen on the 1920 and 1930 censuses with her parents in Frohna. As a teenager, she was quiet but displayed mood swings. After surgery to remove her appendix, she came to believe that she had undergone a hysterectomy. The misconception contributed to a deepening depression, as she loved children and mourned the idea of loosing the ability to have them, which eventually led to violent behavior towards her mother. In early 1934 before she turned twenty-one, her father Theodor made the sad decision to take her to the Farmington State Mental Hospital. She was diagnosed as schizophrenic and lived the rest of her life in an institution, first in Farmington, then at a nursing home in Bel Nor, Missouri, and finally in Chesterfield, Missouri. Her sister Milda eventually became her guardian and frequently visited her. Her niece Sheila Monti-Molina, who also visited her, said, "She did beautiful embroidery, according to my mother." In the photograph to the left, taken at Farmington, she was holding her niece Imogene (Meyer) Unger. She died at age eighty-two and is buried in Concordia Lutheran Cemetery in Frohna.

Photo courtesy of Imogene (Meyer) Unger

73

Raymond Hugo Kaempfe *(September 13, 1917—July 7, 1971)*

Raymond (Ramey) was christened on September 23, 1917 when he was ten days old. In the 1920 and 1930 Missouri censuses, he appears by his given name Raymond with his parents on their farm outside Frohna. During World War Two, on January 7, 1942 when he was twenty-four years old, he was inducted into the Army and was stationed at Dawson Creek, Canada in northeastern British Columbia where he worked with the ordnance Heavy Auto Maintenance Company, doing service along the newly constructed ALCAN Highway, now known as the Alaska-Canadian Highway. That highway is considered an engineering marvel and was completed in record time.

Photo courtesy of Imogene (Meyer) Unger

He returned to Frohna as a Corporal and married Olga Sophia Haertling on January 16, 1944 at the old Immanuel Evangelical Lutheran Church in New Wells, Missouri. She was five years his senior and they were second cousins/one time removed, with Andreas Koenig and Maria Albrecht being their common ancestors. A newspaper clipping from the time described how his bride wore a street length, dusty aqua dress, and she and the attendants including his sister Milda, wore carnation corsages. Eventually, they had two daughters, but one died as an infant. He was godfather to his sister Milda's second child Carmelo Monti in 1948.

Olga Haertling and Raymond Kaempfe
Married January 16, 1944
Photo courtesy of Milda (Kaempfe) Monti Estate

The couple moved to a farm that had been in his wife's family located near New Wells, Missouri, and Ramey became a farmer. His nephew Courtney Meyer, who grew up in Frohna and worked with Ramey for a couple of years as a teenager, said, "Ramey was a tireless worker. He (farmed) both Theodor's farm and his own from the mid 1940's through the 50's," after Theodor's health began to decline, and he made countless numbers of trips between the two farms, often driving the six miles in his John Deere 60 which used LP gas, one of the first of its kind in those days. He had an Allis-Chalmers combine that he pulled behind the tractor. Courtney wrote, "Occasionally, I had the honor of making that trip on my own. I thought I was 'big stuff' going through Frohna—the deep rich sound of the two cylinders 'Pop Pop' of the tractor is still vivid to me to this day."

Ramey loved to hunt. After a big noontime feast on Christmas Day at Theodor's farm, everyone went hunting rabbits and quail. "Grampa's dogs chased rabbits from sinkholes and brush piles so family members could be challenged in their shooting ability." Ramey was an excellent "shot-gunner," capable of shooting quail in flight, so he particularly enjoyed this.

He was an avid St. Louis Cardinal's baseball fan, and he played both fast-pitch-softball and baseball for a league from Pocahontas, Missouri. Occasionally, he, his brother-in-law Alvin Meyer, and Courtney would travel to St. Louis to take in a Cardinal's game and visit with his sister Milda and her husband Charles Monti Sr.. Ramey and Charlie occasionally played fast-pitch-softball together when Milda and Charles came to the Frohna area to visit her family.

Construction of a new Lutheran church in New Wells was important to Ramey. Austrian immigrants founded Immanuel in 1853 after they decided the six-mile trip to Altenburg, across Apple Creek, was nearly impossible to make on a weekly basis. After attending services in their local public school, they built a parsonage (where they also worshipped) in 1856 in the area called Wels, which was named after their hometown in Austria, and eventually that became New Wells. Their ever-increasing numbers outgrew the house, so in 1874 they built a new sanctuary. In 1957, the congre-

Two Boys with Hounds on the Farm—Circa Early 1930s
Raymond Kaempfe age 15 or 16 (left) and Otto Kaempfe age 12 or 13 (right)
Photo courtesy of Imogene (Meyer) Unger

gation realized they needed a newer building, and by 1958, thanks to hard-working people like Ramey, a large, modern brick church took its place, and it still stands today.

He died young, two months shy of his fifty-fourth birthday in 1971, from a brain aneurysm. During his funeral service, a thunderstorm caused the electricity to go off, so the pastor asked the mourners to sit quietly and think about Ramey's life as they waited for the lights to come back on. Everyone did so, respectfully, for thirty minutes, "a real tribute to him." He is buried in Immanuel Evangelical Lutheran Cemetery in New Wells, Missouri, along with Olga who died seven years later. One daughter Betty Jean Kaempfe survives them.

Otto Harold Kaempfe *(April 14, 1920—May 29, 1940)*

Photo courtesy of Imogene (Meyer) Unger

Otto was christened on April 25, 1920 when he was eleven days old. In the 1930 Missouri census, he appears as a nine-year-old boy on the farm near Frohna with his parents and four siblings. By 1940, he was still single and worked as a blacksmith and helper in the Frohna Feed Store. When he died at age twenty, his Missouri death certificate #19189 showed that he was instantly killed after falling sixty feet from a roof after slipping off scaffolding while painting the roof of the flour (or feed) mill and that he suffered a fractured skull at the base. A newspaper article from the period included a few other details. Theobold Weinbold was helping and witnessed the accident. At 10:30 a.m. (on May 29) Otto "was using a regular painter's ladder and had placed it in position on the east side of the building with the hooks over the comb of the tin roof. He had been painting for some time when the hooks slipped and the sliding ladder carried him off the roof. He struck an offset in the building about fifteen feet down, then fell an additional sixty feet to the ground." It continued, "His neck was broken and his skull was crushed. A verdict of death due to unavoidable accident was returned by a jury called by Dr. W. H. Bailey coroner."

Some family members believed the accident was a result of negligence on the part of the feedmill because it didn't provide adequate safety equipment, and decades later they continued to express bitterness over his untimely death. He is buried in Concordia Lutheran Cemetery in Frohna.

Elton Theobold Kaempfe *(July 15, 1922—August 26, 1925)*

He was christened July 30, 1922 when he was fifteen days old. His Missouri death certificate #24644 shows his name to be Elton Kaempfe, born on June 15, 1922 in Perry County, Missouri to Theodore (*sic*) Kaempfe born in Frohna, Missouri, and Lina Koenig born in Cape Girardeau County, Missouri. He died August 26, 1925 due to meningitis complicated by dysentery at the age of three years, one month and ten days. He is buried in Concordia Lutheran Cemetery in Frohna.

Milda Doris (Kaempfe) Monti *(March 18, 1925—April 13, 2008)*

Milda (or Mickey as most people called her) was born on the day of the Great Tornado on March 18, 1925, on the same day when two of her aunts were injured or died. The list of baptisms in the published church record book for Concordia Lutheran Church ends December 1923, so Milda is not shown in that book, but she stated that she was christened there, probably within days of her birth, just like all of her siblings. She recalled her childhood as happy but filled with hard work. All of the children had duties before and after school, but they loved and cared for each other, so the chores were just part of a nurturing lifestyle. She had a pet sheep and participated in the 4-H Club. Active in her church, she belonged to the Lutheran Walther League. At school, she played her favorite sports— basketball and softball.

After graduating from tenth grade at Brazeau High School in 1941, she moved to St. Louis where she worked as a nanny until she was eighteen years old and could go to work in a factory—Carter Carburetor—and there she met Nellie Jane Charlton who later married Salvatore (Sam) Monti in March 1946. They introduced Milda to Sam's brother Charles Joseph Monti Sr. after he returned home from the Navy, and

Milda Kaempfe at Her Confirmation
Circa 1939
Notice the photo folder attributed to "P.J. Lueders, Frohna, Mo" although he died in 1937. Paula and Alvin Meyer purchased his photography studio building in the 1940s or 50s. See page 71.
Photo courtesy of Milda (Kaempfe) Monti Estate

77

Milda Kaempfe Holding Imogene Meyer
Circa 1943
Photo courtesy of Imogene (Meyer) Unger

six months later on July 6, 1946, Mickey and Charlie were married by a justice of the peace in St. Charles, Missouri.

This caused a great row in the Monti family, since he had dared to marry a non-Catholic who was not Italian, but soon enough, Mickey won them over with her sweet nature and the family accepted her. After their first son was born in 1947, the couple disagreed on how to have him baptized—Catholic or Lutheran. After their second son was born just eleven months later, Mickey relented and told Charlie he could have them baptized Catholic. A priest refused to baptize the babies, calling them bastards, until the young couple married in the Catholic Church. Charlie was furious, told the priest to go to Hell, and declared that Mickey could raise her children as Lutheran, which she did. In a letter dated December 22, 1948 he wrote to his "Dearest Darling" Mickey who was in Frohna visiting her parents with their two sons, "You can have the baby's (Butch and Carmelo) baptized (at Concordia Lutheran Church) so I guess that gets some off your mind." Today, the large pink-and-white ceramic water pitcher and matching washbowl that were used during the ceremony remain family heirlooms in Carmelo's possession.

The family grew to six children (five boys and one girl) between 1947 and 1959, and all the children attended Sunday School and were confirmed at Ascension Lutheran Church during their youth. They moved several times, from an apartment on Kingshighway to a flat in North St. Louis on Labadie Avenue and finally to their own home in Shrewsbury, Missouri at 5116 Michael Avenue, where the boys shared bunk beds in a big basement bedroom while their sister enjoyed the home's second bedroom. In the 1960's Mickey went back to work at Carter Carburetor where she assembled automobile carburetors. The skill came in handy in later years as she once astonished Charles Jr. and Carmelo's college roommate by reassembling the carburetor in his car, and she was known to occasionally clean the carburetor in the family's old Cadillac.

Juggling family life and a job was not easy, but she and Charlie worked as a team to manage the household. Late at night, after everyone was asleep, she could be found ironing clothes or scrubbing the kitchen floor. She liked to cook and bake, so the family always enjoyed homemade desserts after big family meals. Nephew Courtney Meyer and his sister Imogene (Meyer) Unger both fondly recall staying with the family for extended periods of time in the summer, recollecting the good times and great food. Mickey was a loving, generous mother to her brood, and all of her children cherish their memories of her. Her daughter Sheila wrote that she "was always a hard worker, but more than anything she was a good mother to her six children . . . Mom was always there." She encouraged her children to attend college, but they were expected to work their way through, which many of them did by spending summers sweating at the American Can Company alongside their father. Three of them went away to school but came back to St. Louis during breaks, always assured of a welcoming home awaiting them. Two of them attended classes in St. Louis and lived at home for as long as they needed.

In 1977, the couple bought a bigger house at 10520 Gregory Court in St. Louis County and converted the small house in Shrewsbury to rental property. Around 1980, Mickey's blood pressure was determined to be unmanageable, rendering her unable to work at Carter, so she began to collect Social Security. She developed diabetes and spent the last twenty years of her life struggling to manage these serious medical problems. Despite this, she was always ready to host big family feasts on holidays and to help her adult children when they suffered difficulties. She traveled to Denver, Phoenix, Seattle, or Central Florida, often flying alone, on trips to assist one son or another who needed help moving a household or to aid another son or daughter-in-law who was recovering from surgery. When son Mark's wife Kathy required numerous hospitalizations, they stepped in and helped to raise their two grandchildren, devoting much of their later years to managing a second household for them, taking them to and from school, and feeding them most days. When Sheila traveled for vacations or business, she could count on her folks to take care of her beloved pet Magie, a cuddly but aging and ill Bichon Friche.

The children appreciated their parents' extraordinary efforts, so they reciprocated in a variety of ways. While Sheila was young and single, she and Mickey took a trip to Hawaii. Carmelo provided the couple with unique vacations to see Boot Hill, Arizona and later, a trip to Hawaii where he lived. Paul and Mike showed them the sights around Denver, Colorado, and Central Florida. Charles Jr. took them on tours of Seattle, Washington, down to Mount St. Helens, and up to Victoria, Canada on the ferry, where Mickey and Charlie delighted in Butchart Gardens. For their 25th wedding anniversary in 1972, the children pooled their resources and bought them their first color television; then for their 50th anniversary in 1996, they worked together again, threw a big party, and gave them a two-week trip to Italy and Sicily—Charlie's ancestral homeland.

When Mickey's kidneys failed, her son Michael quit his job in Florida in January 2006

Milda (Kaempfe) Monti
Age 82-1/2 in November 2007 and still smiling
Photo by Carmelo L. Monti

and moved home to help take care of her and Charlie. Sheila lived in St. Louis and devoted many evenings and weekends to helping. Others pitched in by remodeling an aging bathroom, coming to relieve the primary caregivers so they could have a break, or flying into town for a birthday greeting, just to say, "I love you," in person. After Charlie died in June 2006, Mickey tolerated the dialysis but soon expressed the desire to be with her husband of nearly sixty years. A broken hip and surgery were more than her heart could take. She died of cardiac arrhythmia and end-stage renal disease on April 13, 2008, and is buried in Jefferson Barracks National Cemetery with Charlie. She leaves behind six children, six grandchildren, one adopted grandchild, seven step-grandchildren, and many great-grandchildren.

Regina Gladys Kaempfe *(March 7, 1928—March 12, 1928)*

Regina's Missouri death certificate #10052 shows her name as Regina Glydis (*sic*) Kaempfe, born in Frohna, Perry County, Missouri, on March 7, 1928, to Theodor Kaempfe born in Perry County, Missouri and Lina Koenig born in New Wells. She died at the age of five-days-old on March 12, 1928 as a result of premature birth and is buried in Concordia Lutheran Cemetery in Frohna.

Imogene Meyer's Confirmation April 1955
Left to Right: Augusta (Meyer) Kipping, Lina (Koenig) Kaempfe, Imogene Meyer and Reinhold Kaempfe
Augusta was Alvin Meyer's older sister and Imogene's aunt and godmother. Reinhold was her godfather.
Photo courtesy of Imogene (Meyer) Unger

End of the Century and Into the New Millennium

By 1955, Lina Kaempfe was nearly blind as a result of complications from diabetes and she had cataracts, which the doctor recommended be removed. Daughter Milda Monti took her mother back to St. Louis for surgery, then to her home in Shrewsbury for recovery. Lina was there about three weeks when she had a heart attack and died at age sixty-eight on the day after Christmas. Eight years later, Theodor was eighty-one years old when he had a stroke due to cerebral vascular disease, lived one day, and died the next evening on December 13, 1963 at the hospital in Cape Girardeau. So many people close to Milda died in December near Christmas that each year as the holiday approached, she expressed dread, fearing that someone dear to her would be the next to go. Along with Lina and Theodor, others who died in December included Eligio Monti (1951), Reinhold Kaempfe (1987), and Alida Kaempfe (1995).

Theodor and Lina had four male offspring but none of them produced male children. Two daughters did have sons, but both their last name and their Y-chromosome came from their fathers. Hence, the Kaempfe male bloodline and namesake did not extend forward from Theodor, but it did from his three brothers Otto Gottfried, Wilhelm Friedrich "William" and Carl Johann Kaempfe in Farrar, Frohna, Perryville, and Cape Girardeau, Missouri and Kansas.

After Theodor's death in 1963, his five heirs kept the farm. Raymond continued working it, but he died unexpectedly in 1971 from a brain aneurysm. That year, Theodor's granddaughter Imogene "Imy" (Meyer) Unger, her husband Thomas "Jerry" Unger, and their two sons Gregory and Thomas moved to the farm. Imy wrote, "At that time we started with a small Ford tractor and three head of cattle. Jerry planted corn and soybeans for several years, but then he went to raising beef cattle and making hay." They began making improvements, including digging a large pond that was intended for watering the herd and fishing. One major purchase was a new hay baler that made large round bales. Over time, several Kaempfe siblings sold their shares to their sister Paula. Finally, on March 23, 1978, Imy and Jerry bought the farm from her mother Paula, so it remained in the family.

Once they owned the farm, the couple decided to begin modernizing the house and its surrounds. They remodeled the kitchen and bathroom. Having a well drilled was a big improvement over the cistern, which required water to be hauled in. In 2003, they had vinyl siding installed. Imy wrote, "I painted all thirty-six of the original shutters which my dad Alvin had made for Granma years ago." Over the years, they have painted, wallpapered, re-placed floor coverings, and installed a new furnace and air conditioning. In 2005 they had a double-car garage built near the back of the house. They fenced off a few acres at the back of the farm for a wildlife preserve and their son Tom planted trees and grasses for the animals.

In 2007, the couple decided to sell the cattle and rent the land to a neighbor, who keeps around one hundred head of cattle there. Jerry still drives a tractor—a Zetter with a cab and air conditioning. The wildlife preserve has proven beneficial, as Jerry, their sons and grandsons continue the family tradition of hunting deer and turkey. Imy wrote, "The deer have gotten so brave that I found deer tracks all over the garden last week."

Another major storm affected the farm on May 8, 2009, although not nearly as severely as the Great Tornado of 1925. Winds reached one hundred miles-per-hour and it was designated an "inland hurricane." Several of the farm's outbuildings had roofs ripped off and the barn sustained a lot of damage. About twenty trees were either uprooted or broken. In the year since, they have succeeded in repairing all the buildings. As noted in Chapter Eight, that same storm toppled the steeple of Trinity Lutheran Church in Altenburg.

Imy "inherited Grandma's love of flowers," and maintains many of the same flowering bushes, perennials, and annuals that her grandmother Lina planted, including phlox, mock orange, red honey suckle, peonies and a snowball bush, "covered with beautiful white blooms… the same bush that Courtney and I had our picture taken with Aunt Mickey about sixty-five years ago. Each year when the pale yellow and lavender iris blooms, it brings back many fond memories of Grandma and her beautiful flowers."

Imogene (Meyer) Unger
Spring 2010 - With flowers from "Grandma" Lina on her farm
Photo courtesy of Imogene (Meyer) Unger

On May 1, 2008, Jerry and Imogene were awarded the University of Missouri Century Farm Award, jointly sponsored by the University's Extension program, College of Agriculture, and the Missouri Farm Bureau. Guidelines for the award mandated that the same family must have owned the farm for one hundred years or more; that "family" consisted of direct descendants, which included grandchildren; and that the farm contained at least forty acres from the original land acquisition that still made a financial contribution to the family's overall farm income. They met all requirements after determining that Traugott acquired the farm in 1876. The award is a testament to the endurance and history of the Kaempfe family and their continuing presence in Frohna, Missouri and to those brave German souls who left their homeland and sailed for the New World—their Zion on the Mississippi—nearly two hundred years ago.

A Newer Tractor on the Farm Near Frohna
With the Missouri Century Farm Award Sign
Photos courtesy of Imogene (Meyer) Unger

BIBLIOGRAPHY

This Bibliography contains the resources that were used to construct this genealogy and family history. I attempted to include every book, document, Internet website or person, and any omission of credit is purely unintentional and should not be construed as plagiarism or copyright infringement.

Books

One book in particular stands out as an invaluable resource: *Zion on the Mississippi*. This 600-plus page, well-researched book is packed with many facts and details of the Stephanites' emigration history.

American International Encyclopedia, published by Little and Ives 1954

Concordia Lutheran Church at Frohna, MO published by Perry County Historical Society

Except the Corn Die by Robert J. Koenig, published by Robert J. Koenig, 1975

Grace Lutheran Church at Uniontown, MO published by Perry County Historical Society

Roll of Honor, Vol X, "Names of Soldiers Who Died in Defence of the American Union" published by Government Printing Office, Washington, DC, 1866

St. Clair County, Illinois, Birth and Death Records 1843-1870 published by St. Clair County (Illinois) Genealogical Society

Trinity Lutheran Church Records, Millstadt, IL published by St. Clair County (Illinois) Genealogical Society

Trinity Lutheran Church at Altenburg, MO published by Perry County Historical Society

Trinity Lutheran Church: A Pictorial Souvenir (located in St. Louis, MO) by Dennis Rathert, 2000

Zion on the Mississippi by Walter O. Forster, Concordia Publishing House, 1953

1868 State Census for Cape Girardeau County, MO published by Cape Girardeau Genealogical Society

1876 State Census for Cape Girardeau, MO published by Cape Girardeau County Genealogical Society

Documents, Microfilm and Records

Autobiographical essay "The Life Story of Paula Verseman" March 1990 provided by Imogene Unger

Confirmation Record for Eduard Koenig from Immanuel Evangelical Lutheran Church, New Wells, MO provided by Morgan (Meyr) Lake

E-Mails or letters from Milda (Kaempfe) Monti, Morgan (Meyr) Lake, Cindy (Bachmann) Brigham, Ruth Kasten, Nelson Haertling, Shannon Renee Ryan, Charles Monti, Paul Monti, Sheila Monti-Molina, T.V. Vessell, Eric Kreft, Imogene (Meyer) Unger, and Courtney Meyer.

Death Certificates from Missouri for Milda Doris (Kaempfe) Monti, Theodor S. Kaempfe, Mrs. Justina Kaempfe, Lena (*sic*) Christina Kaempfe, Louise (Kaempfe) Stueve, Charles (*sic*) Stueve Jr., Otto Kaempfe, Mrs. Martha (Gemeinhardt) Kaempfe, Wm. F. Kaempfe, Anna M. (Mangels) Kaempfe, Carl J. Kaempfe, Frieda (Burfiend) Kaempfe, Otto Frederick (*sic*) Oswald, Ernst Kaempfe, Joseph T. Kaempfe, Rudolph Kaempfe, Rudolph H. Schade, Julianna Maltilda (*sic*) Koenig, Wilhelm Edward (*sic*) Koenig, Alwin Koenig, Elizabeth A. (*sic*) Koenig, Benjamin Koenig, Juluis (*sic*) Koenig, Otto H. Kaempfe, Regina Glydis (*sic*) Kaempfe, Elton Kaempfe, Sophia Haertling, August M. Meyr, Gustav Herman Haertling, and Paul Johannes Lueders

Drawing of Unknown Woman identified as Juliana Mathilda (Reuschel) Koenig, scanned and digitally retouched in the mid-1990's by Carmelo Monti, reproduced herein on page 46

Genealogy charts for their family lines from Cindy (Bachmann) Brigham, Nelson Arthur Haertling, Morgan (Meyr) Lake, Shannon Renee Ryan, and T.V. Vessel

Handwritten or typed genealogy lists by Milda Monti, Carmelo Monti, Paul Monti, Sheila Monti-Molina, Imogene Unger and Courtney Meyer

Illustrations of St. Johns Church and the *Olbers* on pages 11 and 13 are from originals in the collections of the Concordia Historical Institute, Department of Archives and History of The Lutheran Church-Missouri Synod, 804 Seminary Place, St. Louis, MO 63105, and are used with their permission. Further reproduction is not permitted.

Illustrations of City Crests for Kleinpestitz, Korbussen, Rippien, and Ronneburg by Carmelo L. Monti, 2009 reproduced herein on multiple pages

Immanuel Lutheran Church (New Wells) records and photocopies provided by Morgan (Meyr) Lake

Ink rendering of Lutheran Church in Korbussen, Germany by Carmelo L. Monti © 2010 reproduced herein on page 57

Ink rendering of Palitzsch Building in Kleinpestitz, Germany by Carmelo L. Monti © 2010 reproduced herein on page 8

Kleinschmidt Cemetery Enumeration, *SCCGS Quarterly*, 1988 #2, pg. 89 to 92

Korbussen Lutheran Church (Korbussen, Germany) records and photocopies provided by Nelson Arthur Haertling; Birth Record for Christina Haertling reproduced herein on page 56

"The Lutheran Witness" Vol. 116, No. 4, April, 1997, p. 7-12, Concordia Publishing House

Letter dated December 22, 1948 from Charles Monti to Mrs. Charles Monti, Box 36, Frohna, Missouri, provided by the Milda (Kaempfe) Monti Estate

Maps that were referenced: *Europe*, National Geographic Magazine; *USGS for Altenburg Quadrangle, Missouri 1949*; and *Illinois* and *Missouri* by Automobile Association of America

Maps of Germany 1815 and Missouri-Illinois drawn by Carmelo L. Monti in 2003 and 2009

Map: *USGS Map Altenburg Quadrangle 1949* segment showing locations of Kaempfe farms prepared by Mary L. Miller in 2003 on page 26

Marriage Licenses for Heinreich Hennecke to Justina Tute and Traugott Kaempfe to Justine Hennecke from Illinois Regional Archives Depository

Marriage License for Edward Koenig to Julia Reuschel from Cape Girardeau County Archive Center, Jackson, MO provided by Morgan (Meyr) Lake reproduced herein on page 44

Marriage Record for Eduard Koenig to Julie Reuschel, Immanuel Evangelical Lutheran Church, New Wells, MO provided by Morgan (Meyr) Lake

Military Service Record, Samuel Kaempfe, National Archives and Records Administration, Washington DC, including Record of Death and Interment reproduced herein on page 20

Missouri Century Farm Logo © 1976 University of Missouri, Columbia, MO (downloaded from their website www.extension.missouri.edu/centuryfarm/ReplacementSignOrderForm.pdf and given permission to reproduce—see copyright notice) reproduced herein on pages 59, 61, and 69

Newspaper articles from unknown newspapers in vicinity of Frohna, MO, provided by Imogene Unger:
"Otto Kaempfe, 20, Killed in Fall" probably dated May 29, 1940
"R. H. Kaempfe Weds Olga Haertling" probably dated Jan. 17, 1944

Newspaper articles from unkown newspapers in vicinity of New Wells, MO, provided by Morgan Lake:
"Alvin Koenig, Farmer of New Wells, Dies; Funeral Rites Sunday" dated Feb. 23, Jackson, MO
"Alvin Koenig Dies After Long Illness" undated

Permanent Record of Birth 1890, Cape Girardeau County, MO State Archives

Photograph of 132nd Marker Flag from New York State Military Museum (see copyright notice) reproduced herein on page 21

Photographs from the collection of Morgan (Meyr) Lake include: Andreas Koenig (page 42) and the Koenig Homestead (page 46)

Photographs from the collection of Mary Miller and Carmelo Monti include: Theodor and Lina (Koenig) Kaempfe 1906 (page 3); Communion Chalice (page 12); Headstones for Christiana Kaempfe, Juliane Kaempfe/Drewes, and Wilhelm Kaempfe (page 18); Concordia Lutheran Church (page 24); Lina Koenig portrait (page 40); Trinity Lutheran Church (page 48); Aerial View of the Farm Near Frohna (page 58); Lunchtime in the Wheat Field (page 64); Milda (Kaempfe) Monti (page 79); and Mary Linda Miller's portrait by Carmelo Monti (page 94)

Photographs from the collection of the Milda (Kaempfe) Monti Estate include: Traugott and Justine (Hennecke) Kaempfe (page 4); Samuel Kaempfe (page 15); Family of Traugott and Justine Kaempfe c. 1900 (page 25); Traugott Gotthilf Kaempfe c. 1895 (page 27); Edward Wilhelm and Juliana Mathilda (Reuschel) Koenig (page 38); Three Kaempfe-Koenig Generations (page 60); Theodor Kaempfe with Hounds (page 63); Theodor and Lina (Koenig) Keampfe 1946 (page 67); Reinhold Kaempfe's portrait (page 69); Reinhold Kaempfe on Main Street (page 70); Paula Kaempfe and Alvin Meyer's Wedding (page 72); Olga Haertling and Raymond Kaempfe's Wedding (page 74); and Milda Kaempfe at Confirmation (page 77)

Photographs from the collection of Imogene (Meyer) Unger include: Theodor Kaempfe with Tractor (Cover, inside cover and page 64); Theodor Kaempfe portrait (page 6); Kaempfe Women (page 28); Sheep on the Farm (page 28); Four Generations of Koenig Descendants (page 54); Kaempfe Farm House (page 61); Cleanup After the Great Tornado (page 62); Lina Kaempfe with Cats (page 65); Kaempfe Family Reunion 1947 (page 66); Family of Theodor and Lina Kaempfe 1931 and 1937 (page 68); Paula (Kaempfe) Meyer-Verseman (page 71); Alida Kaempfe at Farmington (page 73); Raymond Kaempfe (page 74); Two Boys with Hounds (page 75); Otto Kaempfe (page 76); Milda Kaempfe Holding Imogene Meyer (page 78); Imogene Meyer's Confirmation (page 80); Imogene Meyer's portrait (page 82); and a New Tractor with the Century Farm Sign (page 83)

Poster: Reinhold Kaempfe's political campaign poster in Carmelo Monti's collection of family memorabilia

Register of Births 1884, Perry County, MO State Archives

Ship's Manifest Records from National Archives (Kaempfe)

1850 Census for Illinois (Microfilm and HeritageQuest)

1860 Census for Illinois (Microfilm and HeritageQuest)

1870 Census for Illinois (Microfilm and HeritageQuest)

1860 Census for Missouri (Microfilm and HeritageQuest)

1870 Census for Missouri (Microfilm and HeritageQuest)

1880 Census for Missouri (Microfilm, familysearch.org, and HeritageQuest)

1890 Reconstructed Census for Missouri (online)

1920 Census for Missouri (Microfilm, Ancesty.com, and HeritageQuest)

1930 Census for Missouri (Microfilm and Ancestry. com)

Other Resources

Cape Girardeau County Genealogical Society (membership)

Cape Girardeau Archives Center, Jackson, Missouri
IRAD Depository, SIU, Illinois
Latter Day Saints Genealogy Library, Winter Park, Florida
Missouri Bureau of Vital Statistic, Jefferson City, Missouri
Missouri State Archives, Jefferson City, Missouri
Orange County Public Library, Main Branch, Orlando, Florida
PAF5 (Personal Ancestral File 5th generation) software from familysearch.org
Perry County Historical Society (membership)
St. Clair County Genealogical Society
St. Louis City Library, Main Branch, St. Louis, Missouri

Internet Websites

One website in particular played a major role: familysearch.org. Operated by the Latter Day Saints (Mormon), it was invaluable because of its vast resources and broad spectrum of coverage, and it provided the free software program PAF5, which generated the Ancestry, Descendant, and Pedigree Charts. Most websites were first visited prior to 2003 and some have ceased to exist in subsequent years.

General

www.familysearch.org
www.rootsweb.com
www.sos.state.mo.us/arc
www.maps.google.com/maps
www.multimap.com
www.mapquest.com
www.hamrick.com/names/
www.surnames.behindthename.com/
www.ssdi.rootsweb.ancestry.com/
www.findagrave.com/
www.catalog.loc.gov/
www.ocls.info
www.en.wikipedia.org

Kaempfe-Koenig

www.showme.net/CapeCounty/archive/1890-Census.htm
www.itd.nps.gov/cwss/
www.civilwarhome.com/ShermansMarch.html
www.stclair-ilgs.org/stchome.htm
www.illinoiscivilwar.org/
www.dmna.state.ny.us/historic/btlflags/infantry/132ndInfFlankMarkers.htm
www.cr.nps.gov/abpp/battles/nc017.html
www.cyberdriveillinois.com/cgi-bin/archives/marriage.s
www.dresdner-stadtteile.de/Sud/Kleinpestitz/hauptteil_kleinpestitz.html
www.habich-dresden.de
www.heukewalde.de/

www.ronneburg.de/stadt_rbg/geschichte/geschichte.html
www.txdirect.net/users/rrichard/napoleo1.htm
www.maproom.co.uk/maps/th/thlarge.html - map of Thuringia
www.Infoplease.com/ce6/history/A0843822.html
www.bannewitz.de/
www.germanlife.com/Archives/1996/9610_02.html
www.vogelbeck.de/
www.najaco.ru/directory/meaning_names/names_eng/e.html
www.genealogienetz.de/reg/NRHE-WFA/lippe.html#Geographical%20Regions
www.genealogienetz.de/reg/ger1871.htm#preussen
www.genealogienetz.de/reg/SAC/Kirchen/dresden_ev.html
www.immigrantships.net/v6/1800v6/johanngeorg18390107.html
www.saxonyroots.com/
www.thueringen.de/en/content.html
www.atomix.com/haertling/haertling_bio.html#biography
www.jewishgen.org/Communities/LocTown.asp
www.home.bawue.de/~hanacek/info/earchive.htm#BB
www.perrycountyhistoricalsociety.org/index.html
www.rootsweb.ancestry.com/~moperry/queries/surnames.htm
www.en.wikipedia.org/wiki/Dawson_Creek,_British_Columbia
www.lcms.org/ca/www/locators/nchurches/c_detail.asp?C341270
www.antiquefarming.com/john-deere-history-1.html
www.immanuelnewwells.org/history.html
www.extension.missouri.edu/centuryfarm/
www.spreadsheets.google.com/pub?key=pXKdp5LkS_-8OcSSAGBpwfQ
www.fallingrain.com/world/GM/a/P/246/
www.en.wikipedia.org/wiki/Thuringia
www.en.wikipedia.org/wiki/Greiz_(district)
www.en.wikipedia.org/wiki/Ronneburg,_Thuringia
www.en.wikipedia.org/wiki/Korbu%C3%9Fen
www.landkreis-greiz.de/en/tourism_culture/history/indexl
www.landkreis-greiz.de/en/tourism_culture/sights/castles_palaces/index
www.kfvs.com/Global/story.asp?S=10332605
www.tower-rock-winery.com/altenburg.htm
www.altenburgmuseum.org/
www.saxonlutheranmemorial.com/default.aspx
www.immigrantships.net/v4/1800v4/eberhard18521108.html
www.en.wikipedia.org/wiki/Great_Flood_of_1844
www.haertlingfamily.org
www.genealogy.com/users/b/u/e/Robert-G-Buecher/FILE/0044page
www.genealogy.com/users/b/u/e/Robert-G-Buecher/FILE/0053page
www.genealogy.com/users/b/u/e/Robert-G-Buecher/FILE/0059page
www.extension.missouri.edu/centuryfarm
www.extension.missouri.edu/centuryfarm/ReplacementSignOrderForm.pdf

Proper Name Index

Note: Women are listed by their maiden names

ABOUT THE AUTHOR

Reared in St. Louis, Missouri, Mary Linda Miller graduated *summa cum laude* with a Bachelor of Fine Arts degree from Maryville University in 1978; worked for twenty-five years doing drafting and technical writing in the fields of civil engineering and architecture while living in St. Louis, Phoenix, and Kaneohe, Hawaii; and traveled extensively in the United States, Western Europe, and Japan. She currently resides in Orlando, Florida with her husband of over thirty years Carmelo Monti and their son Jason—both Kaempfe-Koenig descendants—and she actively participates in her church and online at www.findagrave.com and www.authonomy.com.

Her writing includes poetry; a technical manual for interpreting American with Disabilities Act Design Standards for the Hawaiian State Commission on Persons with Disabilities; a technical manual for corporate civil engineering AutoCAD drafting standards written in Phoenix; three self-published collections of genealogy and family history; a completed novel *Liminality: The Fox Woman's Child*, which combines Japanese mythology and religion with mid-20th-century American history; a published children's early chapter book *Terry Trackhoe Goes Missing* that was illustrated by husband Carmelo Monti; and a book of photography *An Hour Over Denali* that contains aerial photos of Denali National Park, Alaska. Her poetry, short stories, and photographs appear in three anthologies.

Works in progress are an unfinished sequel *Terry Trackhoe Goes Swimming* and an unfinished novel that combines the Hawaiian mythological romance of Laieikawai with a modern event—Hurricane Iniki—which she experienced first-hand while living on Oahu. Hurricane Charley, which ripped through Orlando in 2004, reinforced that experience, and every hurricane season in Florida reminds her that she still has a story to tell.

Photo by Carmelo L. Monti

www.marylindamiller.com

www.ingramcontent.com/pod-product-compliance
Lightning Source LLC
Chambersburg PA
CBHW081401280526
45788CB00009B/2947